FEEL THIS BOOK

FEEL THIS BOOK

An Essential Guide to

Self-Empowerment, Spiritual

Supremacy, and Sexual Satisfaction

Janeane Garofalo and Ben Stiller
as told to
Ben Stiller and Janeane Garofalo

Preface by Ben Stiller

Foreword by Janeane Garofalo

BALLANTINE BOOKS   •   NEW YORK

A Ballantine Book
The Ballantine Publishing Group

Copyright © 1999 by Smooth Daddy, Inc., and I Hate Myself
Productions, Inc.

www.randomhouse.com/BB/

LIBRARY OF CONGRESS CATALOGING–IN–PUBLICATION DATA
Garofalo, Janeane.
    Feel this book : an essential guide to self-empowerment, spiritual
supremacy, and sexual satisfaction / by Janeane Garofalo and Ben
Stiller as told to Ben Stiller and Janeane Garofalo ; preface by Ben
Stiller ; foreword by Janeane Garofalo. — 1st ed.
        p.   cm.
    ISBN 0-345-41292-3 (alk. paper)
    1. Man-woman relationships—Humor.   I. Stiller, Ben, 1966–   .
II. Title.
PN6231.M45G38   1999
818'.5407—DC21   98-37036
                                                                  CIP

Text design by H. Roberts Design

Manufactured in the United States of America

First Edition: February 1999

10   9   8   7   6   5   4   3   2   1

Table of Contents

Acknowledgments

In the course of putting together a book such as this, there are many, many people without whose help these ideas could not become a reality.

Unfortunately, those people would be too numerous to mention.

There are, however, certain people who must be listed—people who, though they were not in any way involved with the writing of the book, were in every way responsible for it.

First and foremost, Marjoe Gortner, whose inspirational presence both as an actor and orator has been the spiritual cornerstone for the words that grace these pages. Though we have never actually had any contact, Marjoe's message is so close to our hearts that if it were a bullet we'd be in serious trouble. Keep up the good work.

Robert Tilton, whose "Pastor of Gas" pirate video-tape has brought countless hours of joy to millions. On many a late night we would pop the old fart tape in the VCR and find our . . . second wind.

The incomparable Garth Brooks, whose voice and music exist on a plane not many have visited. His soulful pop-country love songs, mixed with a wickedly sly sense of down-home fun, continue to remind us every day what it means to be an American.

Dennis Franz, whose loving performance as *NYPD Blue*'s blustery cop "Sipowicz" has entertained, enlightened, and intimidated us all. We sincerely hope that we never get on your bad side, Detective.

Andrew Ridgely, The other guy from Wham!, whose brave persistence in carrying on long after basking in the light of fame and glory is a walking reminder to us all that life goes on.

George Michael, for the same reason.

Young Jonathan Lipnicki, who has shown us all that we have a wonderful child within, waiting to jump out and entertain millions. Cheers to you.

You are all in our hearts and souls, and though we cannot share in the material profits of this venture—and that goes for any family and so-called friends who would think that we are now quite solvent—we do share in the wonderful after-glow of a job well done!

BEN STILLER

First off, a few disclaimers. I do not presume to be an expert in any area regarding self-help, relationships, personal growth, or anything else that I have been asked to write about. I have no medical degree, I am not a father, and I am not married. Nor do I have my own sitcom.

So what right, say you, do I have to collaborate with my fellow semi-celebrity, the short, spunky (and beautiful-yet-not-aware-of-it) Janeane Garofalo, on a tome that will no doubt end up as one of the last items you see on the way to the register to buy a "real" book?

I honestly can tell you that before the good people at Ballantine approached me about this, I wouldn't have had a freakin' clue. I was quietly pursuing my own rather modest showbiz career.

(More on that later—or, if you can't wait, flip right to the first addendum, "Who is Ben Stiller?")

One day I get a call from my agent (yes, they still call them that), asking me if I would like to write a "funny" book about relationships.

"They want you to do it with Janeane, kind of a 'He Said, She Said' type of thing," he reported. "Only funny."

My first reaction was, "WOW. A book deal! I've been reading about these fuckers in *Entertainment Weekly* for years and now the gravy train has finally rolled into my courtyard! Hallelujah! Sweet Jesus I am going to make some *MAD, DOPEASS FUCKYOU MONEY, MAMA!* Good God, almighty! *YES! YES!* I am in! How much Daddy? Tell me how much they wanna drop in my everwillin' pockets, 'cause I will take every cent and promote the shit outta this beautiful down payment on the MalibubeachfrontretreatslashPorsche911 I have been dreaming about!"

My next thought was . . . No. No, greedy boy Ben.

Let's not enlist in the pathetic ranks of those nonwriters who get huge advances so that they can sell a few books at Christmastime and hit the bestseller list for two weeks before the public catches on to the scam. Let's have a little dignity in a Tiger Woodsy world gone mad with endorsement deals and instant fame. Let's not join in the madness. I called up my representative and ordered him to tell the book people thank you, but no deal. The few "phans" I have (I don't like to call them fans—that is short for fanatics. I prefer "phans"—short for the self-designed acronym "PHANTOMS"—People Hoo Are Nice TO Me) would not appreciate my selling out to Big Brother.

A few days went by and I fell into a deep depression. Things were slow; my last movie had bombed. Everywhere I looked there seemed to be a copy of *Seinlanguage* or *Couplehood*.

Spiraling into a major funk, I did what I usually do when depressed: numb my mind out with television. (Actually, I usually do that even when I am happy.) There was Janeane Garofalo being interviewed by Barbara Walters. Barbara Walters—that's big! Being called a leading voice of her generation. Starring in a movie with Sylvester Stallone. I logged on to the Internet and found twelve websites devoted to Janeane alone. Guess how many I had?

It turns out that my "phans" were just that—phantoms, nonexistent.

The good news? There was nobody to let down! Feeling the weight lift from my shoulders, I called my agent and told him I had changed my mind—that I had made a big mistake. He said it was too late. After the Barbara Walters special, Ballantine was happy to do the book with Janeane alone. I called Janeane and begged her to let me get back in on it. She said she would consider it but she didn't think it was probable—the advance was huge, and, frankly, she just didn't see what I brought to the table.

I told her I was the "He" of the "He Said, She Said." "What are you gonna do?" I asked. "Just 'She Say' the whole book?"

She said, "I don't like your tone. You sound desperate."

I said, "My tone? You don't like my tone? Since when are you the judge of my tone?"

She said, "Whatever. I gotta go."

Then I said, "No, no, no—this is it! This is the book! 'He Said, She Said'! What we're doing is perfect for the book! We can just argue and tape it and have someone transcribe it and edit it!"

There was a long pause.

Needless to say, she agreed, and the fruit of our labor now rests in your hands. And the really wonderful part is that in the journey of discovering what this book was about, the book itself evolved. (Yes, we had many of those arguments, but unfortunately they were not suitable for transcription.)

What transpired was a true journey of self-discovery which led me into realms heretofore unknown to me. One cannot write a book on relationships—even a "funny" one—without learning about one's true self. And this process has enlightened me in areas I never imagined possible. My life has been forever changed.

We started out writing a "funny 'He Said, She Said' book" and ended up uncovering human truths that we never knew were lies. Sound weird? Well, read on. It just gets weirder. In fact, my hope is that this book will actually cross over from the "Humor" category to the "Self-Discovery" shelf. Or maybe even the Sci-Fi section. (I truly believe that ETs do exist among us—and not the fuzzy wuzzy kind. More to come on that.) But I am getting ahead of myself.

Janeane and I have not spoken much during the writing process, but I trust that when we actually do reconnect, probably at one of the numerous bookstore appearances that have been planned for us, we will find that we are both better people for having gone through this experience.

Ben Stiller
Wenokosha, New York
June 1998

JANEANE GAROFALO

Foreword

Why? What in the Sam Hill do you think you're doing? Who in God's name do you think you are? Are you quite insane? How dare you! You're crossing lines with me? Don't you even start! No seriously—who *are* you?

You might be thinking all these things as you endeavor to absorb this book. So let me tackle your primary query: "Why?" In my defense, let me assure you it wasn't my choice. Those of you fortunate enough to know me are aware that I've been channeling a self-help guru for the last fiscal year.

I don't know her name or how the heck she got in. Perhaps someone left the spiritual door ajar. Maybe she found the spare key under the pseudo-rock atop the emotional porch of life. Or she busted the basement window and crept up the stairs of illumination and growth. In any event, for whatever higher purpose, I have been selected to serve as vessel for the "message." I am the humble mouthpiece-hyphen-*"vox humana"* of a supremely gifted, would-be Mensa member who's got a "bone to pick" with the unenlightened.

It's difficult to remember the exact moment this additional *"über vox"* entered my skull, but I do know it was the same evening I attended a record release party on the Lower East Side. At some point during the festivities, a young Betty Page look-alike dropped a fistful of pills into my gin and tonic causing me to panic and flee, leaving my backpack and a bewildered coworker behind.

The unsolicited "cocktail" turned out to be a powerful yet fortuitous "smack in the face." I might never have had the honor of playing host to my new inner "friend" had I not collapsed in a heap outside Benny's Burritos and been rushed to St. Vincent's hospital for a stomach pump. Not only was my gut sucked clean, but the space between my ears benefited, too.

Such is the history of a wise, compassionate entity that dwells above my neck and behind my eye sockets. As you journey deeper into this book-hyphen-guide you'll learn, as I did, the wisdom of the gal I'll call Vox Number One.[1] Your life will evolve and change, and you'll become more effective, likable, and savvy. If not to others, then at least you'll assume you've become all those things—and that's half the battle. You'll realize that all other self-help books by people who sometimes act or do standup comedy are Bunk with a capital B. Let this be your path, your candle, your wake-up call, your compass, your sensible shoes, your rucksack, your nutritional supplement, your Frappuccino©, your spare underwear, your canteen. Suffice it to say, the *tool* needed to negotiate the *outward bound* program we call life. Not everyone will be lucky enough to read this, so it is your responsibility to gently coerce friends and family into *learnifying* or *seekifying* for themselves. I urge you not to *lend* or *share* this blessing with others, as they can only receive the benefit by purchasing. Allow your peers to take that vital first step on their own. If you give them this book, you'll deny them *necessary* motion toward *learn-growth*. (None of the previous italicized words will be discussed in this book.) So make the decision to be "present" in

---

1. Vox Number One guided my pen across the pages of a yellow legal pad lying atop my desk whilst I was in a fugue state. So please do not accuse Janeane Garofalo of being a mediocre writer. Aim all criticisms at Vox Number One or Rachel, the girl who dosed me.

the "roll call" of life. Remember, you can't do it without me, and "good ol' " voice number one. Enjoy us, revere us, and above all, *NO LENDING*.

Janeane Garofalo
Nutley, New Jersey
June 1998

How to Use This Book

This book was written in an attempt to share with you certain ideas and concepts that we, as entertainers and people-who-are-in-touch-with-ourselves, have developed over the years.

Just as swallowing an entire jug of elderberry wine would make you sick and nauseous, yet a few sips with dinner brings a warm happy glow, so, too, it is with this book.

Trying to ingest it all in one sitting—though possible—is not advised. There are too many subtle nuances, tender touches, and hidden messages to be gleaned from a single reading.

Instead, we urge you to pour over this manual, reading and rereading certain sections if they make no sense to you, or if they seem unclear. Chances are if there is something you don't understand, it's because it is something you *need to understand*. If we have used a word that is too big or complicated, get your butt off the toilet and pick up a dictionary. (Or consult Janeane's very helpful glossary on pages 205–210.) Make it your business to make this book part of the fabric of your everyday life.

The ideas and concepts espoused within do work—you just have to embrace them. Only by lovingly wrapping your arms around them and rubbing up real close—close enough that the ideas can feel you breathing on them—will you gain their true benefits.

While we have written this book in the simplest way possible (and if we have done our job right, it will *seem* simplistic and obvious), it is far from that.

As with any document or theory dealing with the human psyche, one must be very careful what one says and suggests, as we are all fragile beings who are easily influenced and manipulated. Both of us have gone to great pains to make sure that we have not knowingly abused that privilege.

We are professionals. Though not specifically professionals in the fields of "psychology" or "psychiatry," we are both highly paid actors and comedians, and as such know more about neuroses than you could possibly hope to imagine.

Feel like spreading the word? Go out and buy ten copies and give 'em to your best friends. Better yet, buy ten more and lay them on your worst enemy. Didn't Jesus say something about loving people you hate, or who hate you (or something)?

Writing this has been nothing less than *COM-PLETELY TRANSFORMATIONAL* for us. All that is left is for you to completely transform yourself and everyone who you have a speaking relation-ship with, by exposing them to the concepts wait-ing within these pages.

As you continue on, be fearless—*change* is not something you need to ride the bus—and know that by the very act of just picking up this book, just looking at it across a crowded bookstore and deciding to impulse buy it, you have sent a resounding beacon to the universe. And it's a message louder than the loudest Metallica concert and clearer than the clearest waters of the Carib-bean Sea.

What is that message?

Turn the page, and let the adventure begin.

Any photocopying, duplication, or other unauthorized reproduction of this book is a federal crime and punishable to the full extent of the law: A minimum of five years imprisonment, a fine of $25,000.

BEN

The Peter (Piper) Principle

The other day I ambled about my garden, picking some scrub berries from underneath a tattered potato plant that has been withering on a vine for many months. Now, my garden is quite modest: a few green bean sprouts, some onion plants that never "took," and a host of other ne'er-do-well fungi and bushes. The garden itself is located in an area behind my house that gets about fifteen minutes of sunlight a day—so right from the start, it's been an uphill battle. Add to the mix a Great Dane known by the monicker of Rex, who also claims the turf as only a Great Dane can, and well . . . you get the picture.

As I embark on this journey of discovery, I figure as good a place to start as any is my own garden. In many ways, a relationship is just like a

garden. In fact, one could say the similarities are almost eerie:

GARDEN	RELATIONSHIP
A garden needs tending.	A relationship needs tending, too.

I can't really think of any more right now, but
hopefully you get the idea.

Another way to go with the analogy is to say
that your garden is really a reflection of who you
are. In other words, if you have a healthy garden,
you are healthy emotionally.

The greener your thumb, the truer your heart.
This would make professional farmers the kings of
good relationships. Now I haven't met any actual
farmers (I'm from NYC, where we still believe in
good old concrete and garbage), but from what I
have seen in movies and TV shows like *Field of*

Dreams and *Green Acres*, it seems to me that those fat o' the landers have their share of problems, too.

So where does that leave us?

Well, right back where we started—staring at my sorry excuse for a potato plant. Somehow I can't help thinking that maybe I'm to blame. Maybe if I didn't plant my veggies where the dog run is, and where there's no light, they might do better. Maybe if I was more attentive it would benefit. Maybe if I actually knew some of the basic tenets of gardening I might be better off.

Too bad people can't look at relationship planning in the same way. Don't plant a potato where your dog craps. It won't taste good. How many times have we met that other person, who we think is going to make us happy, only to give up everything in pursuit of them? And only to end up miserable and alone with nothing after they lead you on and then finally blow you off for someone else? We are, all too often, the poor potato spud to someone's Great Dane droppings.

Only by realizing that *where* we plant our relationship garden is as important as *what* we plant will we be able to fully realize a bumper crop of love and happiness that would make this nation's farming deficit a thing of the past.

BEN

History

HE SAID . . .

Well, if you've come this far, you probably have figured out that this book is exactly what it says it is. A lot of boring old advice on life and relationships.

No juicy revelations about our own personal bouts with drugs, cancer, or homosexuality. If that's what you want, the Liberace bio comes out next month. I joke.

However, it would belittle you, the reader, to assume that you would accept any advice on relationships from two authors who are currently unable to hold one down (a relationship, that is).

Beyond stating that it is none of your g.d. business whatsoever whether or not we are happily treading water in some mutually codependent ocean—which is what most relationships are, in our humble view—and that just because we are not quote unquote "able to have a committed relationship" (whatever that means), there is a qualification that Janeane and I share in writing this:

We have experienced, quite possibly, the worst relationship ever—at each other's hands. That's right—stop the presses. *USA Today*, grab this quote from the excerpt that we publish in *Harper's*: Garofalo and Stiller were once an item.

An item of what, is the question. All I can tell you is that the item was highly perishable and went bad after about twelve weeks. We let you in on this secret for a good reason. It is a prime example of the pitfalls that can plague you in that wonderful cesspool we call love.

We have each agreed to recount the relationship from our own perspectives, not just to show how each partner has a slightly different take on things, but also because we were contractually obligated to deliver at least one "He Said, She Said" type of chapter.

What follows is an honest account of a "real" relationship, one that to this day we both regret wholeheartedly. If the tone is negative, do not be put off. Yes, there is still an awful taste in our mouths, six years later, but that doesn't mean that your relationship will turn out the same.

In fact, for my part, I have tried to incorporate many pointers as to where things went wrong, and what could have been done to counteract what became the abortion of an alliance.

WE MEET . . .

How often have you had a friend who has told you about a girl or a guy they know whom you would be "perfect" for? Such setups almost always fail under the pressure of two people who have been built up to each other, only to be not what they expected.

Janeane was not what I expected, right from the start. I guess I didn't expect her to be drunk. That might sound callous and cruel, but it would be unfair to the reader to paint this relationship in anything other than its true, ugly colors. I know this does not necessarily fit with the "humorous" vein of the book, but you asked for it.

I was at T. J. O'Pootertoot's, a popular eatery in Beverly Hills, for nearly an hour before Janeane ambled through the revolving door—about twice before she figured out how to emerge from it.

By this time I had downed my share of gin and tonics, but I was still sober enough to smell the whiskey on her breath.

Despite her state, she was looking quite good,

apparently on one of her "upswings"—part of a cycle that I would come to know all too well during the coming weeks.

She seemed very eager to find a booth where we could be "alone together," and by the pizza-tizers she was feeling—well, how should I put it?—let's just say "frisky."

Not knowing what I was in for, I played along, finding her boldness attractive, the gin making her all the more enticing.

By dessert, we were both more than a bit tipsy. We were downright sloshed.

On the way to the parking lot, Janeane told me she loved me, and then belched. We made out for a long time in my car, which we somehow navigated back to her house.

Once there, we made messy love and passed out with our backs to each other.

After that, we were inseparable.

Doesn't sound like a fortuitous beginning, does it? But believe it or not, no real mistakes were made until the morning after. In other words, if we had both just left it as a drunken, one-night coupling, it would have been perfect.

But we made the mistake that most unhappy couples do—we threw *good money after bad*.

RULE: NEVER HAVE A SERIOUS RELATION-
SHIP WITH SOMEONE WHOM YOU GET DRUNK
WITH AND SCREW ON THE FIRST NIGHT.

THE PARTY

The first few weeks were a heady time for both of us.
We fell into each other, sometimes quite literally. Under Janeane's influence, I rarely saw a sober moment.

Both up and coming in the comedy world, we
melded together in the way many codependent
couples do. Each reveled in the other's success and
fell into deep depressions when one of us didn't get
a job we wanted.

I was experiencing one such depression around
the time of my birthday. I had been called back five
times to audition for the role of Potsie Jr. for the
fledgling Fox network's pilot *Happy Days '92.*

It was a revamping of the popular series from the
'70s that took place in the fabulous '50s, only up-
dated to take place in the early '90s. The idea was
that Fonzie, now in his early sixties and penniless,
convinces Richie Cunningham, now president and
CEO of Cunningham International Hardware, to buy
the vacant lot where Al's once stood. Fonzie, who
has just been released from the Wisconsin State
Penitentiary, has a dream of turning it into a youth

center. Anyway, I won't bore you with the details. Suffice it to say that Potsie Jr. was a plum role and could have been what we call in the industry a "break-out character." Like an Urkel, or someone like that.

As luck would have it, I was informed that I had lost the role on my birthday. It seemed that the head of the network thought P. J. (Potsie Jr.) should look more "all-American."

I didn't take it well. Perhaps I had had a little too much of certain pharmaceutical substances that I shouldn't have had; perhaps I was just plain bummed out. All I remember is that when I finally got it together enough to show up at Janeane's, I was wasted. I had repeatedly warned her on the phone that I was not in any mood to do anything for my birthday—least of all, to have a surprise party. But when I walked through that door I was greeted by the most mind-numbing shrieks of "Happy birthday!" that you have ever heard. My skull seemed to be vibrating to the point of being about to explode, and then I was inundated by faces of people I hadn't seen or wanted to see in years. It was hell.

In Janeane's defense, I will say that I had not told her that I didn't get the part. She had no way of knowing the depths of my depression that night. To everyone else I was the birthday boy, but to me I was "Not Potsie Jr."

The details of that night are still unclear to me. I remember Janeane being very upset that I didn't interact with the guests—and I have a vague recollection of getting quite upset when I walked into the bedroom and the TV was tuned to the old movie *Heroes*, which starred Henry Winkler. I believe I might have thrown it out the window.

After that Janeane wouldn't talk to me for a long time. But after I found out that the show was not picked up, things got much smoother between us.

In retrospect, she was right. If she had been stronger, she would have realized that I was "transferring" my frustration onto her. But by staying in the relationship, she was sending me a secret signal that said, "It's okay to get abusive when you don't get the part of Potsie Jr."

RULE: NEVER THROW A SURPRISE PARTY FOR YOUR SPOUSE WHEN HE HAS JUST LOST A ROLE TO JASON BATEMAN.

THANKSGIVING

We probably should have called it quits soon after that, but of course we made the same mistake most couples do: We had intense post-fight sex and decided it was time for me to meet her family.

It was nearing Thanksgiving, and Janeane hinted that she would love for me to accompany her to Nutley, New Jersey, to meet her "clan." I had wanted to take a road trip—camping in the northern mountains of Arizona. It's something I do every year around Thanksgiving—a way of saying thank you to that higher power, in a slightly more spiritual fashion than with a can of cranberry sauce and some dressing.

I posed the idea of a wilderness adventure, and Janeane answered in her usual, disarming, straight-to-the-punch manner, "You can camp up in Wazoo Alaska for all I care. *I'm* spending Turkey Day in Nutley with my people."

She hadn't said it in so many words, but the message was implicit: Come with me or else. I got the feeling that if I didn't accompany her, I might be spending a lonely Christmas in the Arizona mountains as well.

I acquiesced, on the condition that we drive across country—which Janeane considered to be a huge concession.

Here's where another mistake was made. Janeane thought she was helping me by agreeing to take a drive when she really wanted to fly. By not *expressing her true feelings*, throughout the entire trip I was subjected to a rippling, roiling, angry little "fly baby" who wanted nothing less than to be laying back munching peanuts on United Air-lines First Class to Newark.

By not communicating her true feelings to me, she subjected us both to a hell ride across the United States in which she was continually cranky, uncomfortable, and hungry. I practically felt like I *was* her father for most of the trip, telling her that we would be there soon and to "keep it down."

By the time the headlights of my fully loaded Aerostar minivan flashed on the Nutley exit sign, I was ready to toss her out, wish her a happy holi-day, and head into NYC for a night of carousing with my old buddies.

By never *expressing her true feelings* to me, Janeane inadvertently sabotaged any chance we might have had for a simple, fun trip.

RULE: NEVER COMMIT TO A TRIP OR VACA-TION WITH A PARTNER WHO ALSO HAS GASTROINTESTINAL ISSUES THAT YOU ARE NOT COMPLETELY COMFORTABLE WITH. (SEE JANEANE'S CHAPTER ON GAS.)

FAMILY TIME

The Thanksgiving weekend in Nutley proved to be a seminal point in the relationship.

I was surely not looking forward to the experience. The tension level between us was thicker than the Delaware Water Gap (which we crossed entering New Jersey), and things weren't getting any better.

The holidays are hard enough to begin with. All the forced "happiness and joy"—the artificial goodwill toward men bullcrap. I would sooner crawl under a rock and hibernate for the six-week period till after New Year's than go and spend endless evenings by the Duraflame hearths of people I don't even know, watching them get drunker and drunker on premixed eggnog from the local Git 'N' Go.

That said, I do enjoy a little Christmas cheer as much as the next guy, and I was looking forward to putting my best foot forward for her family.

Perhaps one of the mistakes that I made—yes, I did make a few in this relationship—was believing what Janeane had told me about her family. I was expecting to find a dysfunctional witch's brew of fathers and aunts and cousins, all abusive and self-centered, not appreciating Janeane for who she really was.

For years she has made us all laugh with her tales of her screwed-up family life and upbringing. How surprised I was to find that these gentle souls could not be farther from the portrait painted in her quite obviously fictitious stand-up act (except for her "nana," who seemed to be in the advanced stages of Alzheimer's—and an easy comedy target).

Right away, Janeane sensed the ease with which her father and I got along, and it became an immediate flash point.

While Pops and I stayed downstairs the first evening we arrived, Janeane stormed up to the bedroom, feeling left out. I thought she might be happy that we were getting along at all, but for some reason she felt threatened.

Her dad and I finished off three six-packs that night, and by the time I wobbled upstairs, we already had nicknames for each other and a date to finish our quarters game the next morning.

Needless to say, I received the literal cold shoulder that night as I slid next to Janeane in her pink canopy bed, just as she had left it all those years ago.

In retrospect, it's all very clear. Janeane's career hadn't taken off at that point, and she was feeling the fallout. Her family being pretty blue collar, they didn't really understand how the "biz" works. All they knew was that she called herself a comedienne yet she didn't have her own sitcom. To put it in the jargon of the technology age, "Does not compute."

Her insecurity about this—along with her general lack of closeness with her dad—had created a tinderbox waiting to blow.

Add to this that her dad and I were about the same height and coloring, and we both shared a love of carpentry and stock cars. Well, that was the match to the fire.

And boy, did it blow. Right about turkey time the next day.

I think I might have said "pass the sweet potatoes" the wrong way, or maybe I laughed too loudly at Nana's incomprehensible babbling. Whatever it was, all I remember is Janeane exploding out of her chair and letting forth with one of her trademark rants, directed at yours truly. She brought up everything from our fledgling sex life to how I cracked my knuckles too loudly at the movies (not a mortal sin the last time I checked).

It ended with me volunteering to catch a ride home on the next flight to L.A. Her cute little cousins begged me not to, as did dad, with whom I had planned to hit the dog track that evening. But it was clear that Janeane was having none of it. I was back in Cali by 8 P.M., partaking of the turkey special at Canter's Deli.

The mistake here was one of mutual enabling. Janeane lashed out at me, also known as *BLURTING*, basically regurgitating all her anger and frustration with herself toward me. In volunteering to leave, I thought I was helping. But in reality I was only supporting her BLURT, reinforcing its effectiveness.

In Janeane's mind, *BLURT* equaled *BEN LEAV-ING*, which equaled getting *her* way. What I should have done, as uncomfortable as it might have been, was let her "blow her wad," as it were. Let her throw all the stuffing she wanted at me, and when it was over, continue on as if nothing had happened. There's only so much crying an infant can do till she realizes she's not getting her bottle.

RULE: NEVER GO INTO A "LOADED" FAMILY SITUATION WITHOUT AN ESCAPE ROUTE—I.E., AN EXTRA TICKET OR VEHICLE TO GET YOU OUT IN A HURRY. I ENDED UP HAVING TO SPEND A GRAND ON A FULL-FARE COACH TICKET—ONE THAT I COULD HAVE GOTTEN MUCH CHEAPER HAD I THOUGHT IN ADVANCE THAT THERE MIGHT BE A "SITUATION."

P.S. She drove the Aerostar back at her own leisurely pace—leaving me wheelless in L.A. during prime party season. Thanks!

THE END

Things settled down when Janeane got back to town. We eventually grew tired of going out to eat alone and called each other. When we first reunited we of course apologized profusely, each claiming the blame for the fight. We both agreed that we needed to communicate better.

About a week into our rapprochement, I got a call from my ex-girlfriend, Melinda. Melinda and I had gone out for over six years and had a totally platonic friendship, except for the time we had sex about a week after Janeane and I started going out. But that was before Janeane and I were really serious. The real mistake there was ever telling Janeane about the meaningless event, which really just served to confirm that Melinda and I were truly not attracted to each other anymore. Janeane held it over my head for the rest of the relationship as proof of my not being trustworthy. Personally, I feel it took great courage on my part to own up to it.

Still, the relationship plodded on for a number of months, both of us awash in a sea of denial. Eventually we even waxed nostalgic about our crazy drive cross-country and the little pet names we had for each other—"Miss Booty Pie" for her and "Abondanza" for me. (In reality we had used these perhaps one or two times, and never sober.)

I should mention that by this point Janeane had gained a few pounds, maybe sixty or seventy. I think this was a result of her feeling very "hungry" for what was obviously lacking in our relationship. I too was hungry, though I fed my own dissatisfaction with treats of another kind, which

I don't wish to elaborate on here. Suffice to say, we were both "out to lunch," both literally and figuratively.

On the occasion of our three-month anniversary, by this time both of us hardly speaking, I made a pathetic attempt to "celebrate." A night at the theater!

The relationship was in effect over, and not even an evening watching the most bestest Shakespeare actor would have fixed anything. The only two people who weren't aware of this were me and Janeane.

The show was called *What the Butler Saw*—one of those interactive dinner-slash-plays where you talk to the characters and go through this big house trying to solve a murder that takes place during hors d'oeuvres.

Things were going fine between us straight through the appetizer. We were giggling at the inanity of the whole thing. There were plenty of suspects, each of whom the audience was encouraged to pick and follow.

Janeane chose "Professor Picklebottom," who seemed to have an airtight alibi—he was "in the loo" at the time of the murder. Yet he seemed to have a suspicious nature, always tapping his fingers on his potbelly and shifting in his old-fashioned wheelchair.

I, on the other hand, chose to follow "Lucretia Lustgarden," who in my eyes was clearly the killer. When the lights went out and came back on, there was "Dilly McDead," deader than a doornail, a candlestick through his skull. (I remember being surprised at the level of realism—it was quite graphic for a dinner-theater show. My hat's off to the special effects team.) And across the room, there was Lucretia, all five-foot-ten of her tucked tight in those spandex leggings and go-go boots, jiggling out the window to the fire escape, wiping blood off her hands.

I wasn't the only one who suspected her—most of the men in the audience followed after me. But I was quick like a cat and got to her first.

Now here's where it all went bad. I had never been to one of these shows and didn't know the rules. But in my defense, I think the actress playing Lucretia bent those rules a little herself, thinking I might swing her a break in the biz.

I followed her out the fire escape and up to the next floor, into what had been decorated as the "torture chamber." Since I was the first up, she grabbed me—let me repeat, *she grabbed me*—and immediately bolted my arms and legs onto a device called the Lonesome Sailor. Now I've seen a lot of torture devices in my day, but this was one I had never, ever come across. It basically lays you out spread-eagle on your stomach, and through a ratchet knob device, the torturer can expand you four ways to Sunday, all while your head is in a steel mask that exposes only your tongue and left eye.

Later the actress was fired. It turned out she was looney. But at the time, I had no idea. When she started the torture, I had to remind myself it was all just a "show"—and that everything would be all right. By the time she pulled off her top and pulled out her resume—well, I was already in such pain from the Lonesome Sailor that my eyes were too watery to even see Janeane when she burst into the room, accused me of being a "pathetic pig," and just as quickly stormed out.

Within five minutes I was in the parking lot, wearing only my boxers and pleading my case to an infuriated Janeane. By that time, it was all over.

No, I should not have put her in a choke hold, no matter how exasperated I was, but it was all so frustrating in the moment. The police who arrived were right to separate us, and though the ninety-day cooling-off period/restraining order was not really necessary, in the end it probably served its purpose.

We had beaten the horse into the ground. This is an example of the way no relationship should end. We had hit our emotional bottom—we had made *Who's Afraid of Virginia Woolf* seem like an after-school special. And we had no one to blame but ourselves.

In trying to make it work, we had surely bitten off more than we could chew—in fact I have Janeane's bite marks on my arm to prove it.

RULE: DO NOT EVER ALLOW YOURSELF TO BE FORCIBLY RESTRAINED IN AN INTERACTIVE DINNER SHOW—EVEN IF IT IS BY A HOT CHICK.

EPILOGUE

Needless to say, Janeane and I eventually were able to become friends again. But it took a heap o' time and a load of understandin'. We actually got together and broke up five more times over the next year, but the details are way too repetitive to list here.

And now, as you read Janeane's account, you will see that two people can have very different experiences of the same situation. I trust you will realize that my description of the events is wholly accurate and based on journal notes and interviews with various friends and family members. While I am sure that what she believes to have happened is in her mind very real, one must take into account all the circumstances and "influences" and above all . . . consider the source.

JANEANE

Herstory

Some incidents in life are blocked out for a reason.

Ballantine Books felt that it was important for the reading public—if there are any of you left out there—to learn more about the origin of Benand-Janeane, *über* couple. Stiller and Garofalo are a force to be reckoned with, and I reckon that you will be more pleased to read about it than I am to relive it.

Apparently some big cheese at Ballantine enjoys seeing yours truly twist in the wind. Ben will also be dredging up our past; his version will no doubt be a creative rewrite of history.

I will say this: Ben and I are a pair of real go-getters who have successfully gone and gotten. We beat the system—we actually get paid to do what we love.

Cosponsoring the Meals on Wheels II program has been tremendously fulfilling for us. Meals on Wheels II has taken the wildly successful mobile food concept one important step farther. Our program still brings food to the needy—but we charge them for it. By encouraging the homeless to pay for their food, we teach them how to take responsibility for themselves. Ben and I then take that money, and spend it.

I was introduced to Ben by a mutual friend, who suspected that we would "hit it off." At the time, merging our extraordinary talent and charisma seemed like a good idea; sometimes two heads are better than one when negotiating with the lady we call "Show Biz." The entertainment industry is indeed a harsh mistress who eats sheltered, upper-middle-class Jewish boys like Ben Stiller for breakfast. He needed me.

Our first date took place in September, 1992. (Being a Libra, I felt it would behoove me to date only in September, while my moon was firmly in the seventh house.)[1]

---

1. Ordinarily, I shun all things zodiacal, but in 1992 I was unemployed and chemically depressed. Therefore, I was open to anything that might offer some comfort. I was also involved in several botched attempts at civic anarchy and received numerous restraining orders. (I like to think that restraining orders are common among seekers and dreamers such as myself.)

We met for cocktails and smart talk at Ben's favorite eatery, T. J. O'Pootertoot's. Ben is fond of family-oriented restaurants like O'Pootertoot's, where "pizza-tizers" are on the house and the birch beer flows in bottomless, frosty mugs. He also enjoys singing along with the mechanical bears and the guilty thrill of tossing his peanut shells on the floor.[2]

"Get a load a me, ain't I somethin'!" Ben would shout when the wait staff presented him with a birthday cake. He pulled the birthday stunt everywhere we went. At first, I was touched by his boyish love of cake, but then I realized that it was a thinly disguised cry for help.

Ben had trouble expressing his needs, and conning innocent theme-restaurant employees into serving him cake was indicative of a much deeper problem. Mustached waiters singing "Happy Birthday" was as close as he came to meaningful interaction with other adults. If he wasn't the focus of attention, Ben just couldn't cope.[3]

After our first evening at T. J. O'Pootertoot's, or "'Toot's" (as we were wont to call it), Ben drove me

---

2. This was a habit resented by many of our friends, who felt it signified a lack of respect for the linoleum tile in their own homes.

3. He mostly socialized with children because, with his lanky good looks, he could easily steal focus from a nine-year-old. Not to mention his dominance in pick-up games of basketball.

home. I was often unable to use my own car because The Club© had become permanently locked onto its steering column. This meant that I could only drive to places which were to the left of my house.

Ben came into my living room for more smart talk, we had marginal sex, and so it began.[4] We had a tumultuous, yet lucrative affair. Working and living together was often fun and interesting. Those were heady times, and we were always on the move. Yet, somehow, I managed to gain seventy pounds.[5]

Was I, in fact, starving—for affection? Was I trying to become some kind of eyesore, so he wouldn't want to "sex me up"? Both theories are open to discussion. The weight issue was a real sore subject for both of us.

Ben was plagued by insecurity and doubt. He didn't want his college buddies to think that he would date a "fat chick."[6] When asked about his girlfriend (me), he would produce the photo that came with his wallet—even if the inquisitor was

---

4. He had an annoying habit of referring to me as "Melinda" whenever we got intimate.

5. Ben often mentioned how slender Melinda Kankarides was.

6. Many was the night I would overhear him muttering in his sleep, or to our sleeping dog, Rusty, "I don't want my college buddies to think I date a fat chick."

someone who knew me or had stated on other occasions that they knew the wallet photo was fraudulent.

I tried to divert Ben's attention from my girth to his favorite subject—himself. Since he liked celebrating his birthday so much, I would organize multiple surprise parties at various eateries and homes.[7] Almost every attempt went horribly awry. The harder I tried to please him, the less pleased he became.

I even started wearing a T. J. O'Pootertoot's mechanical bear costume so Ben would like me better, but after six months the poor visibility grew tiresome and the heavy bear head had damaged my spine.

We spent most holidays at my parents' house in Nutley, New Jersey. But it was awkward because Ben refused to speak to my nana. He thought that she was "stuck up" because she had a sweatshirt and an outsized mug proclaiming her the "World's Greatest Grandma." I tried to explain that they were popular gifts rather than a title she had bestowed upon herself, but Ben would insist that her arrogance ruined his vacation.

I could go on and on about incidents like that, but I'll "cut to the chase" and relate the final

---

7. Recently I discovered that my friends resented donating their living rooms so that Ben could be surprised by my presence behind a couch.

insult—the so-called straw that broke my inner camel's back.

After months of waiting, I was finally able to score us a pair of tickets for the hottest show in town. Interactive murder-mystery dinner theater has always been Ben's favorite, and there was no tougher ticket than this one—the Cadillac of interactive murder-mystery dinner theater—*What the Butler Saw.*

The cast had been enjoying tremendous reviews for the show's entire run. One cast member in particular was generating quite a bit of "heat" in the L.A. basin area. Out of respect for her privacy, I'll call her Goddamn Motherfucker. GDMF played the part of vixen with the authenticity of someone who's graced many a Hollywood mattress. Hats off to you, GDMF, for playing the role of interactive femme fatale so convincingly that Ben actually gave me crabs that very weekend.

GDMF caught everyone's eye, and by the time the Neapolitan ice cream was scooped, Ben was a goner—and I was gone. I sat in the parking lot waiting for him to take me home.[8]

I wound up sitting there for seventeen hours. When Ben finally showed and asked me for some

---

8. I couldn't walk home. The aforementioned bear head–related spinal damage was still fresh.

money, I was confused, hurt, and angry. I suggested that we start seeing other people, and he said he had been doing that all along. "No," I said, "I mean actually dating other people, not just looking at them."

"Oh—I see what you're saying," he said. "I thought you meant literally just seeing other people, which sounds sort of frustrating."

The key word was *frustrating*. I couldn't believe that I had allowed myself to date Ben Stiller, and now I was getting dumped for the female lead in *What the Butler Saw*. So we agreed that in the future we would only meet for professional purposes, or if we were drunk and felt like having emotionally destructive sex.[9]

This book is a product of the first part of that agreement. And hopefully, we can help you in ways we were never able to help ourselves or each other.

---

9. Note to Ballantine: Be careful what you wish for.

JANEANE

Blame the Family

L et's start with Tolstoy and his legendary insight into the horror show known as the family unit.

All happy families are alike, but every unhappy family is unhappy after its own fashion. In other words, decide what your siblings and parents may have done to you and *run with it*. Let's also take into consideration the damage inflicted by familial/ societal/ideological demands such as religion, athletics, and nationalism. Because it takes a village . . . to ruin a child.

Grasp onto the blame and don't let go. The oft-told tale of the monkey with his nut-laden fist caught in the tree is supposed to teach us to release and taste freedom. Wrongo. I say squeeze tighter and keep all the nuts. Do not share; do not sacrifice your hard-earned nuggets of pain and ill will. Letting go is limited thinking.

James Mill believed that "the purpose of the media is to train the minds of the people to a virtuous attachment to the government." Let's extend that to: The purpose of both the American prime-time situation comedy and the Republican National Convention is to train the mind to a virtuous yet unfounded attachment to one's own family tree. Blood may be thicker than water, but it is still sticky, unpleasant, and generally nauseating.

Since the Russian Revolution of 1917 we have faced the supposed threat of communist expansion. In the past, a sitting American president would point the finger at that catch-all evil incarnate known as communism. More recently the brown-skinned desert dweller has replaced the commie as the national scapegoat. As easily as brown erases Red, so too can you rely on theory, myth, and propaganda to focus on a relative and start blaming.

Is it a lusty uncle? An emotionally bereft mommy? Or a dad who lived inside a bottle? It doesn't matter, any port in a storm works fine. Perhaps a manufactured disability or food allergy will suit your needs. Grab a therapist and do-si-do your way through the square dance of upper-middle-class contemporary adult survival. Living in a world of "it's not my fault" and "you're not being fair to me," it's a convenient place to hang your hat.

Just as the above-mentioned communist expansion threatened government interests, so too are your interests threatened by family and certain "friends." Think about it—your dad probably wasn't so unlike Noriega or those Kennedy-era scapegoats Trujillo and Bosch, supposedly minding their own beeswax in the Dominican Republic.

Good God, man. Think about it! Somehow they are to blame, just like your daddy, and Papa needs to be overthrown by a little coup called "recovered memory." It is an effective tool in that it needn't be proven to annihilate thine adversary.

The mere suggestion of guilt infiltrates the minds of a thrill-hungry public. The accuser remains above the law, armed with little more than a sullen expression and a string of bad relationships as proof of any wrongdoing. Dad or Uncle Charlie will be tainted for life, but you will "grow" as a result of their suffering.

Ben's Footnote to Janeane's Chapter:

I just want to say I agree with everything Janeane stated in her short yet very smart-sounding essay. Now I may not know as many big words as she does, but I did catch *communism* and *evil* in there. And all I can say is, Right on, sister! America rocks! We are a free people, and I will defend that right to the death!

For many financially secure Caucasian adults between the ages of twenty-four and thirty-seven, "complaining" about the family is an essential "healing tool" on the road to emotional balance.

Janeane's Footnote to Ben's Footnote:

Ben hits the nail on the head when he calls my essay "smart sounding." Follow my example and dazzle with a multitude of political, historical, and cultural comments. It is not necessary to back up your ill-informed references as most people are afraid to expose their ignorance by asking.

BEN

Faster-Mations ©

THE POWER OF WORDS

A very wise old man once said, "We are the stuff that dreams are made out of." Now, I don't know who this ancient sage was—and undoubtedly he was a very revered and hallowed man, with a long white beard and a lot of "followers" who made him think he was the best thing since creamed corn—but I got news for ya, folks: He was dead wrong.

We are the stuff that *words* are made of. That's right. Everyday, run-of-the-mill, boring old . . . words.

What do I mean? Well, think about it. You're sitting there reading this book. Maybe you're on a subway, maybe you're in the john, maybe you're on a twig near a fig in Galilee, but you are *reading* this now. And though you have never met me, you are experiencing my thoughts and beliefs through this book. My words are influencing you at this very moment, in a way more powerful than you even realize.

If I were to tell you to close this book right now, would you do it? Seriously—I mean it. Close this book, and then open it back to this page. Right now. Don't read another sentence. Really—close it.

CLOSE THE BOOK.

Did you do it? If you're like 78 percent of Americans, you did. That's right—in a survey done by a respected research group, 78 percent of Americans (who could actually read) responded to written suggestion in a positive way, meaning *they did what they were told*. Of those 78 percent, only 22 percent were even aware that they had been *told to do something*. In other words, they just *did* it. Sound familiar, Mr. Nike?

That's right. Those sweatshop taskmasters ain't bozos—they do their research. People are impressionable, people! It's nothing to be ashamed of. We are all human clay balls, waiting to be pressed and prodded, molded and pounded, twisted and tweaked, kneaded and rolled. And, perhaps, even fired and glazed.

Outside of these United States, the stats get even more surprising. When that same experiment was conducted in the Middle East, the response to suggestion was over 94 percent. Starting to make sense, Mr. Suicide Bus Bomber? People do what they are told—especially in hot climates. (People in the Sun Belt were above the median in the American experiment.)

There are two more important pieces of scientific data in the equation: In the same study, when the suggestion was not written but oral, the response rate was even *higher*. That's right—when *told* to do something, 83 percent of Americans (who could actually hear) responded to the suggestion.

In the Middle East, the response was over 1,000 percent. In other words, when they were vocally instructed to do something, they did it at least *ten* times.

Now, obviously *what* these subjects were told to do was reasonable. Nobody was told to jump off the Empire State Building. In the American experiment it was a simple task (such as closing a book). In the Middle East, it was a bit more involved (killing a goat, a relative, etc.).

But the results are undeniable: We are a race of yes-men. The only problem is, *we been sayin' "yes" to the wrong man.*

Which brings us to the last bit of data (I promise, no test at the end!): To *whom* do you think we are more responsive than anyone else? I'll give you a hint. It starts with I and ends with . . . I.

You guessed it. In this study, when the same subjects were told to tell *themselves* to do something, across the board, 100 percent of Americans complied. (Only in the Middle East did the numbers drop off.)

When we tell ourselves something, we believe it. And we do it. So what's the problem, you ask? Americans are can-do folk, you say. We win the Olympics in basketball, we beat the Iraqis, and we overcome the odds and save hostages when there are hostages who need to be saved!

Whoa, whoa there. Hold your patriotic horses a minute, General Imokayyoureokay! I'm not signing up to join the Red army just yet. I have total faith in the mind-blowing strength of this nation's awesome military might, not to mention Shaquille O'Neal's awesome power on the boards (and at the box office). And if there were a draft today, I would be number one in line to sign up (even though I have an irregular heartbeat and would most probably be rejected—both by the army and the NBA).

The problem is that the same inner voice that has driven us to be a world superpower is also what has crippled us spiritually. Do you remember that scene in the movie *The Great Santini* where Robert Duvall keeps tossing a basketball at his son's head until he cries? Well, it's no coincidence that it was a *basketball* he was tossing, or that the guy who played the son was the same guy who was later in *Caddyshack*, and who went on to be the guy on *Roseanne*. Well, actually that *was* a coincidence, and it probably doesn't mean anything. But the basketball thing does mean something. Stay with me here.

If you want to look at it symbolically, angry dad Robert Duvall represents the *voice in our heads* that we listen to, continually pounding us with negative thoughts, an angry basketball filled with messages of insecurity and low self-esteem, forever ricocheting through our psyches like a mad, Earl "The Pearl" Monroe of negativity.

We allow this voice to influence us. We believe its lies as it dribbles around us and elbows us in the groin while the ref isn't looking. We are forced to hold our crotches, doubled over as Mr. Negativity spins and twirls to the hoop, slam-dunking our feelings of self-worth straight through the basket as the buzzer signals the end of the metaphor.

If you've never seen a lick of basketball you probably don't know what the hell I'm talking about, but the message still applies. We are our own worst enemy. Luckily, as the data indicates, we are also our own cure!

STOP LISTENING TO "MR. MEANJEANS"

One hundred percent of Americans do what they are told when they tell themselves to do it. Isn't that remarkable? Just imagine what we could do if we stopped listening to the angry Santini-Duvall, and started listening to . . . oh, I don't know . . . let's say, happy Julia Roberts. Remember her as the lovable Tink to the burly and hairless Robin Williams' Peter Pan? What if you put that positive image in your head, buzzing around with good thoughts, her infectious and spontaneous, wide-mouthed Lilliputian laugh inspiring you to make every situation a positive one?

This might sound a little "sunny side of the street"-ish to you, but believe me, I'm no b.s. (that's "blue sky") artist. I, more than anyone I know, have been at the beck and call of the Mr. Meanjeans in my head for most of my life. I'm talking about dark, dark nights of despair and thoughts of suicide, further exacerbated by what-ever drug of choice I had overindulged in that month.

But it wasn't until I started to examine the data that I have presented to you, and I was forced to fill a chapter in this book on affirmations, that I realized the true possibilities of *telling yourself that everything is wonderful*.

THAT'S AFFIRMATIVE, SIR!

Many self-help books have been dedicated to the concept of the "affirmation." I'm not breaking any new ground here. The power of positive thinking goes all the way back to the ancient clowns of Sumeria, who frolicked on the Mesopotamian plain, wearing nothing but face paint and fig leaves, reminding the kings of the fertile crescent that even though the Euphrates was flooding and their crops were destroyed, all was not lost if they laughed to the heavens and did a dance of joy (and sacrificed their firstborn).

Yes, affirmations work. Just ask Janeane, who has one of the most positive attitudes of anyone I know. So where's the puzzle?

Well, here's another clue for you all: The walrus was an affirmation. What? What I mean is that even the best medicine in the world won't work if you don't take it. And as a nation, we don't like to take our medication. We are all naughty Randall McMurphys, slipping our pills under our tongues, thinking we are beating Nurse Ratchet. Talk about shooting yourself in the psychological foot.

In this culture, we are too busy to take the time to tell ourselves the positive messages we need to hear. Isn't it funny how we always seem to find the time to tell ourselves how lonely, ugly, or fat we are? How much we hate ourselves, our jobs, and our mates? Yes, we always seem to have time for the negative. But when it comes to taking five minutes a day to stare in a mirror and repeat a positive message of love and understanding to the universe, well . . . Sorry, Charlie—only good-tasting tuna get to treat themselves well!

After hours of mulling this over recently, I came up with an idea so simple that it almost seems childlike (always a good sign). What follows throughout the book are simple affirmations we can incorporate into our daily lives. Affirmations that we can repeat *while doing other things*.

No more excuses! You no longer need to take that "extra five minutes" for yourself. Let's be honest—who the hell has an extra five minutes for *anyone*, let alone themselves?

The beauty of these user-friendly affirmations, or FASTER-MATIONS©, is that they take no time, very little thought, and—best of all—they work like gangbusters! Whether it's shopping, peeing, or riding the bus, FASTER-MATIONS© will help you achieve total consciousness before you can say Swami Satchida-whatever.

Remember, these are to be done while doing specific tasks, so don't mix and match. For example, doing a URINATION FASTER-MATION© while masturbating can send a confusing message to the universe—not to mention your underpants!

URINATION FASTER-MATION©

As I release my urinary fluids into this bowl
So do I release all thoughts of wanting, need, or envy
As my liquid waste flows out of my system,
So does my anger, hate, and pain flow out into the uni–
    verse.
Flush! Flush! Flush away all bad things! (to be said
    while flushing)
As I release my pee
I am Free! (Repeat three times.)

Addendum for Men Living with Women:
As I lift the seat
So do I lift my light to the universe
And as I close it when I am finished
So do I assure myself
Of not having the anger of the universe—
Or my spouse—
Rain down upon me.

JANEANE

I Love You—
Sovereignty Is Mine

The desire to obtain total control in any relationship is an appropriate impulse. Heed the whine of your inner child's need to take the ball and run home if others won't play along. Consider it your manifest destiny to expand your sway not only over people close to you, but over those you may only glance at in step class. Stretch those manipulation muscles so that they may encompass and/or crush those who don't see your ideological views.

This type of "my way or the highway" thinking can only empower you and edify those in your ken. Why not start your own theoretical kibbutz (but not, theoretically, in Israel). Consider your peers to be your very own kibbutzniks but always take their opinions, or kibitzing, with a Morton's can of salt. Leaving your ears open to the suggestions of others only clogs the mind's eye, thereby creating a type of spiritual glaucoma.

Excessive democracy can be irritating and confusing. I've always enjoyed the secret victory of being right about almost everything; therefore, it is only proper that I indoctrinate others. Orwellian utopias better suit my particular gift for leadership.

A few of you reading this text may enjoy the same omniscient quality. Even if you don't, it's not wrong to act like you do. The most important person to control is the person you have sex with. First and foremost, this person's will should be quickly and quietly slipped beneath your own. Your goal should be to know what he or she is thinking at all times.

To aid me in my quest I've hired a crack team of scientists, intellectuals, and "can-do" types. This group of the bestest and brightest are in the process of developing a high-tech chip that I will eventually implant into the cerebral cortex of my boyfriend's head. It will slide discreetly beneath the brainpan where it will do my bidding and avoid detection.

With this device I will record his thoughts and feelings—an extremely practical investment, as it can save years of gratuitous upheaval, insecurity, and humiliation. I will always have the upper hand, since I possess the gifts of anticipation and clever retort. The upper hand is an important concept to hoard on your journey to spiritual renewal. Trite-isms like "penny for your thoughts" or "you seem a million miles away" will go the way of the gramophone as the Enlightened Relationship 2000 comes to fore.

The chip will provide you with partner access and the ability to negotiate preemptive strikes. Naturally I won't burden my significant other with the knowledge of my installment; that would be defeatist. The chip will allow him to see me at my best: informed, confident, and domineering. In the past, relationships have been bogged down by disagreements and unwelcome surprises.[1] One never had time for mystery or the ambiguities of falling in love. Courtship can be a nasty, all-consuming business.

Grasp the future by the scrotal sac and be a Nostradamus in the game of love. For more information, please send all donations to:

Head Chip 2000
PO Box 972
Terra Haute, IN 02937-4102

---

1. i.e. clashing over movie rentals or marrying a homosexual.

Remember, it is in your best interest to be the iron fist within a velvet glove. Benevolent despot is the role you *deserve* to play when it comes to controlling lovers, coworkers, and friends.[2]

Don't get caught with your vulnerability down around your ankles. Enter the new millennium with the state-of-the-art manipulation hardware. Sleep the sleep of the just while your partner makes a feeble attempt at hogging the blankets.

---

2. Had the chip technology been available during my courtship with Mr. Stiller, I believe we would have surpassed "The Sonny and Cher Comedy Hour" in both ratings and hit singles.

FASTER-MATION WHILE USING THE A.T.M.©

In a loving and benevolent universe, I place my card into
    this machine.
And as I enter my own personal identification number,
I enter kind and benevolent thoughts into the space-time
    continuum,
with the supreme wish that no one has glanced at that code,
which is so simple and unique in its own simple way.

And as I pull my cash from the automatic teller,
so do I automatically draw all the wealth that the uni-
    verse has to offer—
a never-ending wellspring of goodness and harmony
that gives and gives with no end . . .
A service that this cash machine unfortunately fails to
    provide on the physical plane.

And as I wait for my printed receipt,
I wait for all the wonderment and beneficence of this
    reality
to shower me with love and understanding.

And I pray to the wonderful god-being inside us all
that I am in no way harmed as I walk to the safety of
    my vehicle.

BEN

Failure Patterns—
Or Why the Heck
Do I Keep Falling into
That Giant Hole in the Street!?

I f you had a pattern for a suit that was too long in one arm, too short on one leg, and way too tight in the waist, would you have the suit made? Would you have hundreds, even thousands, sold and distributed to unwitting customers?

Of course not. You would throw away the misshapen pattern and start again—or perhaps you would get out of the rag business altogether. Mayhap you might get into new technologies, or better yet, the mail-order business (more on that later). The point is, a bad pattern is a bad pattern. You scrap it and start again.

Well, it seems that a lot of us would make better tailors than human beings. We know how to fix a sport coat, yet we can't fix *ourselves* for all the tea in China.

The Germans have a word for it, *Badentinking*. The French call it *Mal du Paterne*. In any language, it is simply repeating an action that leads to misery, over and over, so that we find ourselves wondering, "How in the bejesus did I end up here—again?"

We all do it—drive ourselves down the dead ends of life's roads again and again, even though the sign ahead says "No Outlet."

How many times have you told your significant other that you would remember to pick up something for dinner on your way home from the office, and next thing you know you're at an all-night eatery with some hermaphrodite you found on the strip, having eggs and bacon at three in the morning?

The point isn't whether or not it's "wrong" to be with a hermaphrodite. Everybody's got their own bag, just like Papa. But there's gonna be hell to pay in the morning, because you weren't honest, and a certain special someone was left high and dry eating Golden Grahams and watching the boob tube till you ambled in with your underwear in your briefcase at half past four.

What would be the solution? Tell your mate about your illicit tryst and risk throwing a perfectly comfortable situation to hell over a meaningless roll in the hay with Lypsinka? Of course not!

But don't say you're gonna be home with grub if you know your hormones are gonna drag you out for a little walk on the wild side! You must accept the reality and adjust. You know you might be late, so call up and *lie*. Break the pattern.

We continually create *patterns* for ourselves to *fail*. These are also known as *Failure Patterns*.

Janeane and I have already let you in on our aborted relationship—a poster child for the *failure pattern*.

Those of you who have a little bout with the bottle know whereof I speak. Drinking is one of the biggest *failure patterns* around.

In the course of my really extensive research period for this book, I spent a lot of time at anonymous twelve-step programs, watching and observing these strong and courageous people who have taken the bull by the *cojones* and decided to say, "Hey, I don't want to continue with this *failure pattern*, (or *Failya Pata*, as the Japanese call it), I want to fix my life!"

I befriended one such hero, a young man of about twenty-one years, whose story is a continuing drama. And though it has no "happy ending" anywhere in sight, it is worth telling.

SEAMUS

My young friend is an out-and-out alky who's really screwed up his life. His name is Sean

Dempsey (yes, Irish—big surprise!). But let's just call him Seamus for our purposes.

Seamus told me his story one day over a Shirley Temple at Pete McManus' pub in New York, the home of many a fine drunk for over a hundred years. (By the way, if I sound callous, it is because I am using a method called "Tough Love"—a proven technique in combatting alcoholism. Sean—I mean Seamus—has since cleaned up his act, thanks in part to my being rude and nasty with him.)

Seamus had been drinking since he was five years old. His first shot was slipped to him at the family breakfast table by his red-nosed father, who told him it would "make his Lucky Charms *really* magical."

Every night his father, who was a policeman, would come home and open a bottle of whiskey, laying down by the television to polish it off while Seamus sat at his feet, tinkering with a fiddle he found in the closet. His father enjoyed listening to Seamus screech on the instrument, patting his head with one hand and telling him he was a good boy while tilting his bottle back with the other. In his young and confused mind, Seamus associated the violin, whiskey, and television with his father's love.

When his dad died of liver failure at the age of forty-three, Seamus found himself sitting alone in front of that television, with his own bottle of whiskey and the fiddle. The only thing that was missing was dear old dad.

Seamus, in his already alcohol-deadened mind, was continuing a *failure pattern* that his father had continued from his father, and so on and so on, all the way back to the Great Potato Famine of the nineteenth century, which is generally believed to be the time that the Irish as a nation began drinking, due to the fact that they were upset about not having potatoes. (Note: I myself can attest to this potato-liquor connection. Being half Irish and half Jewish, I find that I am genetically predisposed to getting toasted and pigging out on potato latkes).

By the age of eighteen, Seamus was a two-fisted Jim Beam man, working as a roadie for a traditional Irish dance band. After the shows, they would retreat to the nearest pub, where they would usually close the place down, singing songs about the Blarney stone and Dublin.

When he was twenty, the band broke up over a name dispute, the leader wanting to call the band "The Mighty Celts" and the rest of the group preferring "The Celtic Mites."

Finding himself without a job, Seamus continued to go to the pub every night, a *pattern* that felt comfortable to him. There he had the television and whiskey, and a bartender who smelled a little like his father used to.

Things went downhill from there. His *failure patterns* dragged him farther and farther into an alcoholic abyss. Eventually he sold his violin for a bottle of booze, and found himself broke and homeless, dancing jigs on the street for pennies.

Seamus says he knew he had hit rock bottom when he awoke one morning in the county jail. Much to his surprise, he was wearing a puke-stained leprechaun outfit with holes cut out in "strategic" places, and his bright red hair had been shorn off, save for two fiery locks where a devil's horns would be. Across his forehead was a black block-letter tattoo that read "Naughty Naughty Lad."

That was about a month and a half ago. Most of his hair has grown back. But the more remarkable difference is that Seamus has broken his biggest *failure pattern* by stopping his drinking. In a rehab in South Boston, I recently asked him how he had done it.

In addition to a renunciation of his Irish heritage (Seamus informed me of the staggering statistic that over 98 percent of people with red hair are Irish, and that 99 percent of *those* are alcoholic—giving evidence to the theory that all stereotypes are rooted in reality), he also told me a parable he had learned his second day in " 'hab" that he credits with pulling him out of the vicious circle of his own *failure pattern* and into a place called hope.

Now mind you, he was still detoxing when he first heard the story, so it's probably not word perfect, but the message is clear.

"The Hole in the Street," as Told by Seamus (transcribed directly from my tape recorder)

Okay, so there's uh, this guy. And he walks down the street and he falls into a hole. Yeah, okay, and then he uhh . . . y'know he gets really pissed, right? Like, "I can't believe I'm in this stupid hole, man! Fuck!" So it, like, takes him a really, really long time to get out. And he finally does, and he's all dirty and shit. And he's all, like, "Screw this shit, man."

So then I think it's, like, the next day, and the dude's walkin' down the same street, okay? And the fucker falls in the same hole! Only like this time when he's fallin' he goes "Damn! I'm fallin' down this dumbass hole again!" But y'know, this time the dude's *aware* of it? Okay? Like he knows he's fallin' down a hole, even though he's still royally pissed and shit.

Okay, lemme see. *(Thinks a moment.)* Yeah! Okay, so the same fucker's walking down the street. But this time he, like, *sees* the hole, but he's, like, got too much forward momentum or some shit and he's in the fuckin' hole again. But at least he saw it.

(Longer pause.) Oh, and, yeah, he tried to, like, step around it also.

All right so, then—lemme see, he falls in, he falls in but gets pissed then . . . Okay . . . uh . . .

(Longest pause yet.)

I, like, forgot some of the times he falls in the hole, but he's like—like every time he goes by the hole he keeps getting better and better at not falling and becoming more like, better at not . . . y'know . . . falling in, or whatever? And then, like, finally . . . *(At this point Seamus grins knowingly.)* And this is the awesome part . . . He like finally decides to . . . he just, like, goes down *a different street*. Get it? He like doesn't even wanna *deal* with the fucking hole. I think, that's like, you know . . . like, go down a different street, fucker! Yeah!

I thought that was *fucked up*! That really got me in touch with a lot of my own shit.

In his own special way, Sean—I'm so sorry, *Seamus*—brings home the simplicity with which we can transform our lives. In breaking his own *failure pattern*, Seamus and people like him continue to inspire me every day.

I raise a toast to you one and all, and salute you in your bravery.

JANEANE

I'm Just Not Myself

Obviously being the best *you* that you can be is important, but let's not forget how vital it is to make a good first impression. The best "you" probably isn't good enough, so let's just go with the best version we can create.

Consider, for example, a facade that might lead him or her to think you are either an incredibly easygoing, roll-with-the-punches kind of "When life gives you lemons make some type of beverage"–type of guy or gal. Or a somewhat artsy, drunken, intellectual, sardonic, Dorothy Parker–trading-witticisms-at-the-Algonquin sort. It's your choice. I like to vacillate betwixt the two archetypes.

I find that both of these personalities, while being essentially false, are best serviced by alcohol.

Upon first meeting someone and pushing forward with the relationship (especially if it's against your better judgment), it's always nice to try on personae and passions. As for ignoring your inner voice in matters of the heart, please continue to do so. It has gotten you this far and perhaps provided you with some particularly memorable—if not downright tawdry—nocturnal experiences.

When dating, it is okay to borrow mannerisms and convictions from others in your social circle or on television. Pilfer quotes from novels, magazine articles, or political figures.[1] C-SPAN, MSNBC, and Comedy Central are fertile ground for the acquisition of cocktail party intellect. It is important that you bob and weave your way past any bullshit detector that a more savvy dinner date might have in his or her employ. Luckily for you, there is no shortage of John/Jane Q. Publics with a limited capacity for exuding or noticing special qualities, real or otherwise manufactured.

---

1. "This country is blessed with a rich supply of coal. It is not the invention of any one man; it is God's gift to the people of America. It requires human labor to dig the coal and bring it back from the bowels of the earth so it may be used for the benefit of mankind."

Fiorello H. LaGuardia
Mayor of New York City, 1934–45

Please note: It is important that you be discussing the anthracite miners' strike of 1925 for this quote to be appropriate.

Think about all of our revered societal icons and the mediocrity will fall in your lap like a gold-plated, lead-bottomed People's Choice Award.[2]

I'm glad I brought that up. Let's talk more about Mr. and Mrs. Public. (Your average person wouldn't recognize a sublime entity if it attempted to fist fuck them while waiting in line for the next Batman sequel.) This regrettable lack of admirable qualities will work in your favor. It's always easy to bamboozle people who feel most comfortable with the familiar. Occasionally top-forty types find mild eccentricity pleasing, especially if the eccentric is wrapped in an attractive package. (This is true of most things.)

It is advisable when dating another average Joe to indulge in the grape or, better yet, the brown liquors. After acquiring a sufficient buzz, feel free to loudly give your opinion about things of which you have only the most tenuous grasp. Regurgitate sound bites from an admired coworker (if that's possible).

When borrowing opinions, craft your sentences in such a way as to sound spontaneous. As for physicality, please raise your glass in a cynical, resolute manner and take a swig while seeming to

---

2. It'll hurt, but we're comfortable with the pain because it's familiar, well-liked, and they "get it" in Iowa.

ponder something. Still waters that *possibly* run deep are good enough. You'll want to seem like you can hold your liquor, so lay down a good bread base before parking your fat ass on a barstool. This may be a tough one for you ladies, who wouldn't be caught dead carbo-loading pre–pint-o'-Guinness.

Some people would rather reach the maudlin, tear-soaked, dry-heave-y-jeebies phase on a first date then indulge in a smart pita pocket at 7:00 P.M. Please remember when raising yet another toast that you cannot retrieve the messages you leave on his or her answering machine after you part company. Put some thought into it and make that 3:30 A.M. plea funny (and I mean funny ha-ha, not funny strange). This is where borrowing a persona or quote from a humorous friend will aid in prolonging the con. It is always better for your date to remember you as "that psycho who was sort of funny."[3]

---

3. There's no glory in being just a *psycho*. Strive for companion adjectives like "brilliant," "artistic," "talented," or "moneyed." With these bonus traits come quasi-interesting lovers who think that they can "change you." Without them, you'll get mates who are bigger losers than you.

FASTER-MATION WHILE SMOKING©

In a loving wondrous cry to the universe,
I light this cigarette with a fiery light
And in so doing ignite a flame of creativity within my
    heart.
And as I drag upon its filtered end,
So do I filter out all thoughts of bad and angry things.
And as the smoke fills my hungry lungs,
So does my hungry soul fill with joy and light and love
    and more joy.

I fill the room with smoke,
Just as the benevolent love light of an all-knowing
Godwomanbeing fills my earthly vessel with God-
    womanbeing love.

Addendum for Cigar Smokers:
As I puff on this round thick roll of tobacco,
I create a feeling of trendiness and fadishness
That reminds the universe that I am living here! Now!
And I am reminded not to judge my actions in the moment,
For they will surely be judged many years hence.

JANEANE

How to Build
a Relationship
on Next to Nothing

rrational crushes, infatuations, or obsessions. Whatever you want to label it, it's important to reach out to others. It is also important to learn how to create something out of nothing. Fabricating reciprocal feelings is good for the self-esteem.[1]

You have, no doubt, heard the oft-recycled adage, "It's impossible to love another until you can love yourself."[2] I disagree. Love, hate, or indifference toward oneself is an irrelevant factor in the

---

1. Just pretend he/she likes you. Pretend really, really hard and you'll start to believe it. Once you're a believer, you'll feel like there's a reason to shower and shave. When you have a reason to shower and shave, you'll feel better about hauling your formerly hirsute carcass out of bed in the morning.

2. If you deny ever hearing that, I would say you're just being contrary. While I endorse devil's advocacy as a clever tool in the art of manipulation, I have no patience when it is aimed at one of my own statements.

desperate search for a connection. I do not use the word *"desperate"* lightly, as "desperation" is a concept-hyphen-entity more forceful than almighty God when it comes to dating, mating, or as it's called in the Bible, "unabated suffering."

While it may be difficult to enter into a healthy, egalitarian relationship whilst marinating in a quagmire of self-loathing, it is a mere can of corn to devote twenty-three hours of your day to obsessing over someone who may only be vaguely aware that you borrowed the Metro section of his or her newspaper at Starbucks. No matter—New Age movements have been built upon less weighty occurrences. You *can* build an affair out of imaginings and desperation.[3] Look what the savvy militant with a vivid imagination can do with a jar of manure, some glycerin, and a little elbow grease . . . *Kaboom boom boom* goes your heart!

Let me again stress the importance of alcohol in prolonging or creating drama. I personally have made a career of building mountains out of molehills, so it's convenient that I live in Hollywood, where people in the entertainment industry are paid to do so on a daily basis.

Let's say you've targeted your future significant other and imbued him/her with all the won-

---

3. That old chestnut!

derful traits he/she has never even thought of pos-
sessing. You've already creatively visualized what
it's like to have sex, bask in the afterglow, argue,
reconcile, and thrive together. Fucking, fighting, and
frivolity—what's left but fruition? (Remember, al-
literation can be important in books like these.)

All of the pining and plotting is essential to divert
attention from yourself and important matters that
relate to your job or your education. It's not illegal to
devote the small part of the human brain that actually works to longing for a mate who remains stead-
fastly unimpressed by you and all the fraudulent
personality traits and "coincidental" meetings you
offer. Their indifference is like mother's milk fortify-
ing your inner mewling infant.

The abundance of goodwill we extend to those
who care little for us would make Ralph Reed blush
and tinkle in his velour panties.[4] It is truly inspirational to see the ladies forgive a multitude of unre-
turned phone calls and severed plans. Modern
technology allows us to check answering machines
from noisy bars so we can lament a barren voice
mail system. After a healthy dose of keening and
moaning, we can then do shots, increasing our desire to hear from that elusive someone. This pining

---

4. I felt compelled to have the reader conjure Ralph Reed soiling his
panties. Perhaps it's an irrational distrust of organized religion or the
fact that he never returns my phone calls.

perpetuates the myth that the indifferent Mr./Mrs. Right is all the more perfect for you.

Goals are good. They are well serviced by repetitive, obsessive thoughts, which act as loyal diversions. While distracted from actively participating in (post–message check) conversation, you are likely to overlook the attention of another. As you ignore the person, he or she becomes attracted to you—thus perpetuating a Chekovian syndrome.

Remember, we wouldn't want to be a member of any club that enthusiastically throws down the welcome mat. And as long as I am recycling adages, try this one on: "It is better to have loved and lost than not to have loved at all." Since when? It is my firm belief that it's better not to have rolled those dice than to have them unceremoniously tossed on the compost pile with the remnants of your pathetic arteries.

Rejection is inarguably one of the bigger pains in the ass experienced by young and old alike, but it is more profound for the youngish and aimless with too much time on their hands. When you're shuffling your Doc Martens into a cafe, movie theater, or booze hut for the thirty-seventh time this week, phrases like "need some space" or "too tired to go out" imbed themselves in your anvil, stirrup, and hammer,[5] where they proceed to rattle and raise

---

5. Hard-working bones (see the chapter "(Don't) Listen Up").

doubts you already harbored about yourself. If it feels like rejection, it is—and you have every right to blow it out of proportion. If they really liked you, "sleep" and "space" would be unnecessary.

Friends shouldn't try to dilute your feelings of romantic hopelessness. Avoid peers known for their honesty; that's not what you need now. In any "normal" relationship, efforts to be alone and slumber shouldn't present themselves until month five. If the requests are made within the first trimester, reach for the Bushmill's, because it's going to be a long, bumpy infatuation.

Drinking and thinking is a healthy way of exercising your capacity for self-induced anguish. Don't forget to repeat the same anecdotes about your potential suitor to whomever will listen. Checking your phone to see if it's working is also a good way to see how desperate your actions become while waiting for a call that probably won't arrive. Endurance is the key to building a better you.[6]

---

6. If you have ever been accused of Narcissistic Neurosis, then you know all about this kind of tenacity. Statistics show that most Americans who suffer from N.N. reside in New York, Los Angeles, and Miami. These cities have designated special smoking areas and highway lanes to accommodate the afflicted.

(NOT PLATO—BEN)

The Cave

Much has been made in recent years about the need for the Man in society to find himself. Robert Bly, Iron John, Jack or Jimmy, it seems that Men are now expected to put on loincloths and bang their hairy chests to the heavens just to prove they are, in fact, real Men. Well, I guess I come from another school of thought—the one where you have to wear shoes and a shirt to get in.

Now I haven't read any of these manuals for manhood. Quite frankly, I'd rather spend the time at the gym or the Turkish steambath near my house. But from what I hear, these books seem to make much of the need for man to go back to the primal urges of the Original Man.

One such book uses the metaphor of "the

cave"—the need for men to be able to have a space for themselves and to totally dominate that place. (Obviously, this concept would be rendered moot if Janeane had her way and implanted her problem-solving dominance chip into every man's cranium. But since that technology is, quite thankfully, far from being a reality, I'll continue.)

But here's where I and the macho-minded gurus part company. They say that you should designate an area or room in your house as the "Cave Space"—a den, a playroom, or possibly an office. Here you are allowed to do whatever you wish: drink beers with your buddies, watch the "game," or just do pottery. Hey, this cave thing sounds real exciting.

Now, as I've said before, I don't claim to be an expert on anything. But it seems to me, if you're interested in getting in touch with your OG (Original Guy), you are not gonna coax him out by cracking a few cold ones in the remodeled basement/rec room. That's like tryin' to get a newt outta the pond by paintin' yer ass green and bending over (as they say in the South). It just doesn't work.

It seems to me there's a much more straight-forward approach. Don't build your own "cave"— build your own *cave*! Yes! It's like that movie *Altered States*—you know, the one where William Hurt took all the drugs and hallucinated in the isolation tank until he actually grew an ape foot in the shower? Now I'm not encouraging drug use of any kind—that is entirely up to you—but the lesson to be learned from that movie is that if you wanna turn into an ape man, you gotta get the man outta the ape! You must create an environment for yourself totally devoid of outside, contemporary influences.

Now I know you're probably saying, "Hey, Ben, I just wanna have an inner growth experience and get in touch with my feelings of maleness—I don't wanna grow a hairy sixth toe, for Pete's sake!"

Well, relax about the toe. That was only a movie. But that's all you *can* relax about. You wanna get in touch with maleness, you gotta act like a male! Get off your lazy modern-day butt, pick up a stick, and write this shopping list in the dirt. If no dirt is handy, pen and paper will do.

You are gonna build a cave, mister!

Here's what you'll need. Depending on the type of cave you want, you'll require a bunch of different materials:

Mud. This is for the musty, American Indian sweat-lodge type of thing. Not technically a cave, but still very earthy.

Rock. This is for a more traditional echo-chamber-y type of getaway. What we think of when we think *cave*. Probably the way to go, but practicality will prevent all but the truly dedicated from actually following through.

Linen. Now hold on. Let me explain. All too often the word "cave" has the connotation of a dark, dank hole that is wet and slimy, where people go to die. Well, welcome to the turn of the millennium, folks! A cave can be a wonderful summer collage of sweet smells, comfortable pillows, and a general unzip-your-pants-and-get-fat feeling! The linen cave is for the man who doesn't need to get his fingernails dirty to prove he is a man.

Once you've selected your material (and combos work, by the way—but be careful with mud 'n' linen), you'll need to figure out a shape. There are a number of possibilities here. Natural caves are usually underground, with bats and stuff in them. My first image of a cave was probably from *The Flintstones*, a semicircular opening to a cavernous yet generally clean interior. I would advocate this. If you are not an architect (I'm not), then you won't know how to make an arch that supports itself. Don't try. I thought I understood the whole flying buttress theory from a special I saw on A & E, but believe me when I tell you it's much more complicated than it sounds.

You are best off getting someone who does not

have much money but does have building experience to come and help you. Offer them what is a modest amount of remuneration for you but what would seem a fortune to them. Then try to "inspire" them to stretch themselves creatively. If the person has any actual cave-building experience, you're obviously way ahead of the game.

You're probably saying, "I thought the point was to build my own cave." You're right. But the point is also that we do not live in the Stone Age anymore, and one of the realities of being a modern man is that we must accept our own limitations.

Once your cave is done, you can kick back with a sense of accomplishment that few men can feel these days. Sure an ironworker can come home from work feeling pretty satisfied that he had a big day working iron or whatever, but how many men do you know who can answer the question, "What did you do today?" with, "I built a cave, my good man."

The answer: not many. You will join an elite group once reserved for bipeds who lived over thirty thousand years ago.

Use your cave to get back in touch with simple pleasures:

• Walk barefoot, even naked, in the cave. Experiment touching your body to different textures in the cave. This might sound risqué, but truly, how many times in your life have you actually placed your buttocks on cold shale? That's a fine top-o'-the-mornin', lemme tell ya.

• Scream really loud—it will echo in a very spooky way (except for in a linen cave).

• Do your own cave paintings. Interestingly, I have found in my own experience that if you actually try to draw really well, they will probably come out worse than the old ones.

• Bring that special someone in there, "take off the gloves," and get prehistoric!

• Have "Cave-Ins" where you invite a bunch of buddies over and get prehistoric!

• Pretend you are the only person on Earth and stay in there as long as you possibly can. My personal record is forty-eight days, but I cheated. I brought Vicadins and chocolate!

The point is to do *any damn thing you want*. It is your cave, and you can dwell in it as you please. There are no rules in cave life. The point is to be a man in a cave. You don't need me to tell you what to do—the directions were included in your DNA!

ALCOHOL FASTER-MATION©

*In a spirit of wonder and awe of the beautiful universe,
    I lift this liquor to my lips and wash away all
    thoughts of negativity and things that are not fun
    to think about.*

*As the alcohol content raises in my bloodstream, so does
    my higher power raise itself to accept the love of
    the cosmos.*

*I choose to imbibe the nectar of loving forgiveness and
    gratitude, just as I choose to imbibe (whatever wine,
    beer, grain alcohol, or malt liquor you are drinking).*

*I rejoice in the lack of pain that I feel, giving in to the
    wonderful godbeingplan that I have no control over.*

*Spinning, spinning, I pass out in the perfect knowledge
    that I am completely unaware of my surroundings,
    and all will be forgotten tomorrow.*

JANEANE

Tomorrow, Tomorrow . . .

Procrastination is the indispensable foundation supporting a vast structure known as "your time." Twenty-four hours, seven days a week, every week, all year long, it's a broad canvas waiting to be filled.

The key word is *waiting*. Procrastination allows you to accomplish the bare minimum within the scope of your waking hours. Put off until tomorrow what could easily be accomplished today. If today is the first day of the rest of your life, then life's too long for adherence to deadlines and societal restrictions. You want it when? Well, you'll get it when it's done.

Your "inner warrior"[1] needs to know that

---
1. The inner warrior is not to be confused with Vox Number One (an audible entity) or the leftist light spirit (or "feelsation"—see page 168). The inner warrior does not fit inside my head or under my epidermis. (FYI, your epidermis is showing.)

he/she can make or break his/her own deadlines. After attending several conferences on time management and "warrior channeling,"[2] I've decided that assignments can wait and warriors are evasive yet somehow pushy little spirits.

In 1969 I began an arduous journey through the American public-school system.[3] Aside from an introduction to a multitude of germs and personalities, I was also greeted with a list of responsibilities. The idea was to mold young people into dependable, educated adults. The result was stressed and rebellious drinkers.

As college commenced, a new cadre of bacteria and seemingly insurmountable syllabi flew in my face. Here is where my yet-to-be-named inner warrior started complaining. His need not to do the reading surpassed the professors' needs to have it done. I listened to the calls of my inner warrior and triumphed. He showed me how to borrow other people's notebooks and Xerox the notes. He taught me how to creatively skip classes and utilize those

---

2. The time-management and warrior-channeling classes were mandatory night school courses I attended in order to avoid prison. [Don't ask.]

3. Just how arduous? See "Intermission Statement: A Denial of Self-Indulgence."

hours learning about "hang time."[4] Heed the calls[5] of your warrior; he/she will show you the ways of procrastination and of performing to the minimum of your capacity.

People who are chronically punctual and get things done rapidly tend to be the objects of office gossip and derision. No need to put yourself in that position. To preserve your self-esteem, stay on the side which *does* the gossiping. Everyone likes a person who is equi-efficient and similar in shortcomings. Let Shakespeare hold the mirror to society—you keep your light under a bushel, and everyone will get along fine.

Heed the warrior's call to put off making credit card payments, taking medical exams, and giving wedding gifts. Similarly, ignore all pressure to go and see a friend's new baby. What if you don't feel the urgent need to spend a Saturday seeing said infant? Anyone can have a child—just give it nine months. How about this: When you finally see one of my films, I'll see your "little miracle."

You need to feel free to make your own timetable. Not unlike smokers, compulsively late, sickly

---

4. Note to father: The money you spent on my tuition was not completely wasted. I learned just enough "big" words and references to hold my own at cocktail parties and on Tom Snyder appearances.

5. You may also receive calls from your own head vox or voxes. You might want to add another line.

student loan dodgers make more interesting dinner companions. New Year's resolutions exist to be ignored. They are like moths bonking their heads on the bulb, a soothing reminder that with a flick of the switch, darkness ensues and the problem is solved.

The same flicking gesture can be utilized on your brain. By January 17, the warrior has conveniently swept the New Year's resolution under the "rug of life." The warrior relieves you of your cumbersome nicotine patches and gym memberships. (Perhaps it's your manifest destiny to expand in the coming year.) The warrior will guide you swiftly past full-length mirrors. Do not fear the ubiquitous student loan or credit officer. Trust the warrior; he protected you from the Columbia Record and Tape Club.

If the phone bill is not in your name, then relieve your mind of its burden. At present, I am grappling with the subject of computer literacy. I have been sorely lacking in software and cyber-skills. The warrior warns me that learning something new at my advanced age could be dangerous. I've decided to set aside the next one hundred years as a possible time frame for compu-learning or getting on-line.

I recommend that you plan on tackling certain tasks in the twenty-first century. This will give you an opportunity to ease into change and event without upsetting the delicate balance betwixt you and the millennium.

BEN

Tupac vs. Deepak

Deepak and Tupac. Shakur and Chopra—two completely opposite philosophies, two lives so divergent. Both incredibly influential figures in our current culture. And both completely unlinked to each other.

As I sat pondering Chopra's latest book the other day, I was struck by what a kind, innocent face he has. I was also struck by the small black print under his name on the cover: Over One Million Copies Sold. This fella knows how to move product. I made a note to myself to check the publication date of *this* book—best not to go against the powerhouse. I called my publisher, who informed me that Deepak is "very prolific" and that there was a good chance our book would be in competition with his. Hmmm.

Deepak and Tupac. One unsolved murder, and one bestselling author who has spent more than enough time as a seemingly "Teflon" guru . . .

I decided to start asking some questions about these two, just to be more informed. What followed was a frenzied couple of months of research and interviews—questions that led to more questions and answers that seemed to lead to other questions. And more answers to those questions that eventually led to answers that seemed to—well, quite frankly—scare people.

It turns out that these two have much more in common than anyone thought. Mind you, what I present here is pure conjecture and in no way influenced by my wanting to "taint" Deepak Chopra in any way. I merely present some interesting facts, and a few "theories." The rest is up to you to decide.

THE TWO "PAKS"

One was a self described "thug," a poet of the streets, a genius who was taken down by the dangerous lifestyle his music espoused. He became the voice for a generation of disenfranchised minority youth, who have turned him into a mythic figure.

The other is a healer and master of human potential, who is still very much alive and has become the voice for a New Age generation of disenfranchised . . . New Age types. He has become a mythic figure to many, especially in the entertainment community, who crave a philosophical teacher and aren't into gangsta rap.

Yet while these two men are seemingly so different, when one looks closely at their backgrounds and works, there are many similarities.

THE NAME

Here is perhaps the most startling of all the similarities. Deepak and Tupac, Chopra and Shakur. Not only do they sound alike, their literal translations are very similar:

Tupac Amaru, translated from its original Inca, means "Shining Serpent."

Deepak, translated from Indian, means "Derek" in English. The name "Derek" is most closely associated in this country with "Bo"—truly a "shining serpent" in terms of her tempting effects on the male population in the mid- to late 1980s. One would assume that the subconscious nature of this is not lost on Dr. Chopra.

Shakur, directly translated from the Arabic, means "thankful to God."

Chopra, translated from the Indian, means "One

who Chops Ra"—Ra being the ancient Egyptian sun god. So, in essence, his surname connotes an act of heretical blasphemy: chopping up the sun god. Once again, we see a disturbing subliminal meaning in Chopra's name. An almost angry response to Shakur's "shining serpent who is thankful to God" is Chopra's "Bo Derek the temptress who chops the sun god Ra."

Here already, there seems to be some sort of a connection between the two, even though Chopra was born many years before Shakur.

Note: Interestingly, however, when Chopra is asked his age he replies "I forgot," which would call into question exactly when the good doctor was born, and whether there might be some correlation in their birthdays.

Their Background

Tupac Shakur was born and raised on the mean streets of Harlem and the South Bronx. His family then moved to Baltimore and eventually to California.

He dropped out of high school and started selling drugs when he was seventeen.

Chopra was raised on the mean streets of

New Delhi, where his father was a prominent cardiologist.

In a shocking coincidence, both men were in theater groups as twelve-year-olds—Tupac in the 127th Street Ensemble in Harlem, and Deepak in the Bombay Babies Children's Repertory Company. And both men starred in their respective company's production of *Jesus Christ Superstar*—with Tupac playing Jesus, and Deepak as a reportedly rockin' Judas. This is Chopra's last known association with organized religion (and musical theater).

Shakur had a rocky road with his family, not having a father figure and being thrown out by his mother when he was seventeen.

Not much is known of Chopra's early years in India. Those who have stepped forward from his childhood say that he was a formidable figure in his neighborhood, and that he had not yet discovered the ways of "spirituality and balanced living" as a young toughie on the streets of New Delhi. Instead, according to some, he was feared in his part of town, calling himself "The Healer." He was famous for his "physical experiments in the mind-body-pain threshold" that he supposedly carried out on the other youngsters he knew, often borrowing his father's medical tools.

RUN-INS WITH THE LAW

Both men suffered many legal scuffles, though Tupac's have been much more well publicized.

Tupac was arrested for taking a swing at another rapper in 1993 and was sentenced to ten days in jail. This would be the first of many jail sentences, culminating in a charge of sexual abuse in New York. He was sentenced to hard time at Riker's Island. In October of 1995, Suge Knight, CEO of Death Row records, posted a $1.4 million bond, and Tupac was released.

Deepak, who by this point had enjoyed much success with his spiritual mind-body-healing teachings, was also arrested in early 1993. It was at a "Freeing Sexual Chakras" seminar in Redondo Beach, California. During a demonstration of the "Sixth Chakra Release Method," local police arrested Chopra and his assistants on indecent exposure charges. The charges were later dropped, and Chopra was bailed out by Demi Moore. Though there is no physical record of any of this happening, many intimates believe that is the result of a very successful experiment in "Sesame Oil Memory Extraction" that Deepak was using. The method makes people forget stuff, like what that thing in *Men in Black* did, only using sesame oil and foot massage—an all-natural mind neuralizer.

Another thing that many people do not know is that during the one night he spent in jail, Chopra wrote a rap song. Up to that point, he had been enjoying great success with his books on healing and well-being. But Chopra wished to "Create More Affluence" in his life, and a recording career is what he was visualizing. Some believe his motivation was not financial, but an actual love of hip-hop. Some say he was (and is) just a frustrated crooner, going back to his musical theater days in India.

Whatever his motivations, soon after his release from jail, he recorded the gangsta-style demo "PATH 2 LUV." He shopped the tape around, the first stop being Tupac's label, Death Row Records. Aparently he was met with ridicule from the hardcore execs there.

Those who know Deepak intimately say he never got over what he considered a personal rebuff from Tupac—though Tupac himself probably never even heard the demo.

This is the only known time that the two ever had anything near an interaction, but some believe that might have been enough. Enough for what?

CHOPRA'S BOOKS AND TUPAC'S RECORDS

If one examines a chart of Tupac's records as they relate to the release of Deepak's books, one could almost argue that Chopra was, in some way, responding to Tupac with his writings. It seems clear that Deepak's titles are all majorly influenced by the rap style. Any one of his books could potentially be the name of an album.

Also, is it truly a coincidence that the Chopra book *Restful Sleep* was scheduled for its third printing just two days after Shakur's slaying?

TUPAC ALBUMS	DEEPAK BOOKS
2POCALYPSE NOW	Quantum Healing
STRICTLY 4 MY NIGGAZ	The Return of Merlin
THUG LIFE	Perfect Digestion
ME AGAINST THE WORLD	The Way of the Wizard
ALL EYEZ ON ME	Perfect Weight
THE DON KILLUMINATI: THE SEVEN DAY THEORY	The Seven Spiritual Laws of Success
—(Tupac gunned down)—	Restful Sleep (3rd printing)

It is also worth noting here that the possibility of a secret "dissing war" between Chopra and Shakur is not entirely implausible. What many people are unaware of is that the guru community is as cutthroat and competitive as the gangsta rap world. While the East Coast–West Coast feud is well known, many people are unaware of the turf wars that have taken place in the San Diego area between Anthony Robbins and Chopra.

Both men base their respective empires out of the sunshine-bathed community. Any residents who live in the area know that if an SUV or limo from Robbins' compound comes anywhere near Chopra's, it will be pelted with rounds and rounds of vitamins and mineral products and potentially lethal bottles of OptiAge skin care cream.

Likewise, if one of Chopra's vans bearing his "colors" of burgundy and black passes into Robbins' territory, it stands the chance of actually being "hijacked" into his compound. There, the passengers might be subjected to a humiliating "paintdown"—literally being painted with Robbins' trademark tooth whitener—and released back to the Chopra compound, to be displayed as a lesson in what happens when you don't "Live With Passion."

THE KILLING

Tupac was gunned down in Las Vegas on September 7, 1996. He had just watched the Tyson-Seldon fight and was driving with Suge Knight to a club.

All that is known of the killer is that he or she drove a white Cadillac with California plates.

Where was Deepak Chopra on the night of September 7? Well, the last place anyone would put him was at a heavyweight boxing match. Deepak's commitment to nonviolence is very well documented. However, there were many other celebrities at that fight, not the least of which were the talented Bruce Willis and his lovely wife at the time . . . Demi Moore.

What is also well documented was the purchase of a white Cadillac El Dorado by a man named Titus Okuru only three months prior to the shooting. While this might not seem very remarkable, it is worth noting that Mr. Okuru purchased the automobile in cash from a dealer in the township of Escondido, only a stone's throw from La Jolla—ground zero for Chopra's operations. And while this still might not seem remarkable, it also worth noting that Mr. Okuru, a resident of Flaming Hills, South Dakota, was in town for one reason—to experience Chopra's "Skydancing Tantric Sex Revelation Weekend."

What does all this mean? Is it possible that these are just a series of obscure coincidences and bits and pieces of information that haven't even been verified? Yes. Perhaps Deepak Chopra was nowhere near the scene of the murder—while no one has asked Chopra if he has an alibi for where he was, one is sure he could easily "manifest" one.

After carrying out my admittedly short investigation, I choose to believe otherwise. It is quite possible that Chopra sees the parallel connections in their early lives as a "Karmic Destiny." Or perhaps he manufactured these in a desperate need to justify what was in reality nothing more than simple hit-record envy—the one ailment that all the ancient Indian healing techniques in the world could not fix for the once–Bombay Baby Deepak.

There are some who would refute that and go further, positing that Chopra and Shakur conspired to fake Tupac's death. Who better to help facilitate this than a doctor trusted by millions, who has a huge organization that one could "disappear" into and start a new life?

One possible benefit of this plan would be a future best-seller penned by Chopra in which he "channeled" Shakur's songwriting/rapping spirit (with Shakur as a true *ghost* writer). This book, perhaps entitled *Tupac to Deepak—A Gift of Love*, would have enormous profit potential in the CD,

CD-ROM, and video crossover areas, not to mention fulfilling Chopra's longtime performing desires. How's that for a VH-1 *Behind the Music* special: "Deepak raps while Tupac naps." (Also, the "Pop Up Video" potential would be enormous.)

Wherever the truth lies, it is important to bring to light these questions, however ridiculous and unfounded they may be, if only to remind us that sometimes Self-Help Gurus are far from perfect. And if they aren't perfect, maybe one should think twice before buying their books.

I'm just saying, that's all. No agenda here.

JANEANE

Intermission Statement— A Denial of Self-Indulgence

At this juncture, let me address the notion that some cynics out there may say that a book cowritten (and/or channeled) by "entertainers" is merely an exercise in self-indulgence. Allow me to silence the critics by stating that I would never attempt to tackle the written word if I didn't think there was a huge global audience eager to read more about me.

I'm extra super-special, and uniquely qualified to reach out to the masses. I am, in fact, *obligated* to connect with those less cerebral than I. As I travel throughout these United States delighting audiences, I find that most people are not nearly as charming or intellectual as I would like. Because of this unfortunate condition, it is incumbent upon me to impart as much of my sublime wisdom as

Ballantine will allow. Collectively, we all benefit from my book deal.

I realize that most people educated within the confines of the American public school system are wary of books. Citizens often report feelings of confusion and anger when forced to read. John and Jane Q Public may feel stymied or intimidated by my intelligence, but the medicine will go down a lot smoother if they just accept that I am their mental superior and I care about them. I did not actively solicit a book deal, nor did I provoke the pierced club kid[1] who "dosed" me. Perhaps she sensed that I needed to clear my third eye, "take a trip," lose my wallet, and weep inconsolably in a public rest room.

All of the above contributed to my rise to role model status. The young people who look to me as a leader flatter me with fan letters and candlelight vigils held outside the house, where I was born a Libra in 1964.[2] I'm proud of my target demographic, but with that pride comes a burden. This burden is not mine to bear, it's yours. As my fan, you have a responsibility to accept all my work unconditionally.

---

1. The only time I ever kissed a girl. She was right about the tongue stud.

2. The new tenants respectfully ask that chanting and prayer requests be kept to a minimum.

The alleged self-indulgence is a smoke screen created by the naysayers and malcontents who populate this once-great land of ours. These wrong-headed miscreants would have you believe that I don't have a right to my soapbox.[3] These are the same misanthropic underachievers who have yet to contribute anything meaningful to *Spin* magazine or The Lifetime Channel.[4] See the connection?

It's not wrong, dear reader, to idolize me or wonder if I'd approve of your lifestyle choices. Music, hair, and degree of denim-fade speak volumes about a person.[5] Don't get caught with your hand inside the acid-wash easy-fits. Learn from me. Vox Number One and I can aid and abet a life well led.[6] After thirty-three years negotiating life's lemons, I've earned the right to dole out some "enlightened lemonade"—and it ain't just pee-in-a-cup, folks. I've seen it all, done it all, and—like country legend George "No Show" Jones—I've lived to tell about it.

I spent the first twenty years of my life attending

---

3. Soapbox: Could be construed as a pejorative term, but I'm 5' 1". Therefore, I often need something to stand on.

4. Television for women.

5. If said person smokes cigars or places a tie around his head when drunk, then approval is invariably denied.

6. Possible bumper sticker slogan. Other choices include "I (heart symbol) my English Terrier" and "No Fat Chicks."

the school of hard knocks, otherwise known as upper-middle-class suburban New Jersey. It was always difficult finding something to do, especially on weekends and summer vacation. Frequently my peer group was recreationally bereft, especially if no one was "holding." I did not have my own phone, and the television in my room was colorless and devoid of cable. Need I even mention the conspicuously absent remote control?

I was the only kid in the cul-de-sac who was forbidden to use her mother's credit cards. I was not permitted to ride in cars with strangers offering candy. This denial of rides and treats left me feeling empty and unloved. Adding insult to injury,[7] my breasts came in far too pendulous and early. This unwelcome development simultaneously destroyed my posture and the ability to maintain eye contact with the boys in my class. This gender-related myopia left me feeling empty and unloved.

Girlfriends' fathers suddenly took an interest in what was "on my mind." Their level of interest increased proportionately to the number of cocktails consumed. Who's afraid of Virginia Woolf? Not me—it's her husband who's likely to introduce fear and loathing to a young girl's psyche. On the heels

---

7. A timelessly dangerous combination.

of those unsightly mammary glands came their regrettable partners in crime—the curse otherwise known as "The Curse"—bad skin and fatty tissue. The upside to this aesthetic assault: your personality is required to pick up the slack and do damage control. The downside: everything else.

Have you ever had a relative touch you inappropriately?[8] Whom are you going to discuss that kind of foul play with? As for me, it was 1976 and everyone was busy decorating their bike for the bicentennial. (To this day the sight of tricolored bunting[9] causes a hysterical reaction. I do not mean hysterical as in humorous, like a spit-take or a pratfall. I mean the other kind of hysterical that can land you in the archives of general psychiatry, under the heading "As yet unrecorded hysterical reaction to a seemingly harmless piece of patriotic material gathered and draped for the practical purpose of decorating a platform.")

If my disclosure thus far hasn't convinced you

---

8. Mandatory inclusion for all books written by or about people who have been on television, under statute 73 dash A of the California literary penal code. This law was enacted shortly after the Loud family made their cinema verité debut on the Public Broadcasting System. Ratings went through the roof and the theater of dirty laundry was launched. Failure to include a mention of "fondling" may result in a hefty fine and up to seventy hours of community service.

9. Bunting's two-tiered impact. See the chapter "(Don't) Listen Up."

of my particularly unique and harrowing journey through hell, then fasten your seat belts. It is difficult to relive the past, but as I write it down I feel the healing start.

In 1982, my senior year of high school, I was forced to ride the bus. The new car I'd received for my sweet sixteen was recalled due to a defective sun roof mechanism. I was then disappointed a second time when my replacement car was vandalized after I left it unlocked in front of the home of an acquaintance that lived on the "wrong side of the tracks." My last year of high school was tainted by the daily commute tearfully endured on a stinky bus.

I was "denied acceptance" yet again when the college of my choice declined to enroll me. But I was learning quickly how to survive. After my father paid my tuition at a different college, I eventually graduated, having switched majors thirty-seven times. I'd like to think I gained an understanding of what Gauguin[10] felt when he painted "Where do we come from? What are we? Where are we going?"

Every time I changed majors, I asked myself similar questions. So I took this thirst for meaning with me when my grandparents sent me to Eu-

10. As you have noticed, there is no shortage of pretentious references in my writing. I want to show my parents that paying my tuition was not like "throwing money in the goddamn street."

rope. While in Amsterdam I was fired from my first job for (and I quote) "throwing the plates away instead of washing them." Harsh treatment for a girl forced to share an apartment with three other people. I returned home and after a few months found another job. I was promptly fired for napping under the winter coatrack. My boss failed to realize that becoming a prophet is exhausting.

Bloomingdales' loss is your gain because coarse living made me stronger. After my boyfriend's father paid the rent on my new apartment, I decided to devote myself solely to things that made me happy. That kind of focus and dedication molded me into the generational mouthpiece I am today. I deserve the pedestal you've placed me on, and if that's self-indulgent, then I guess I'm just old-fashioned.

I came up the hard way. I've summered in Nantucket and skied in Aspen. The value of these experiences is almost too profound to mention; suffice it to say I came down the black diamond slope wiser than when I gondola-ed up.

BEN

Creating All the Money You Could Ever Dream Of

I want money! Ooh ooh!
Gimme money! Ooh! Oooh!
That's what I want, oooh yeah!
        —Popular rock tune

"How much is that doggy in the window,
Daddy?"

"More money than we got, Sugarpuss. Now be
a good girl and hike your skirt up a little more. If
we're gonna hitch that ride back to Reno and strike it
rich, you gotta show a little skin. They ain't gonna
stop for me. That's right. Hike it up real slow and
nasty-like."
        —Popular adult film

Money. I'll tell ya, just the word itself gives me ants in the pants. You ever notice how often we use it?

Money.

Money market.

Money is the root of all evil.

Money makes the world go around.

Money talks and we all know what walks.

Good *money* after bad.

Jesus beat up the *money*changers.

Mo' *money*, Mo' *money*.

Or how about the popular phrase from the cult movie hit *Swingers*: You are *money*.

Try saying it real fast:

Moneymoneymoneymoneymoneymoneymoney-moneymoney . . .

Now try saying it backwards:

Yenomyenomyenomyenomyenomyenomyenomy enomyenomyenomyenomyenomyenomyenomy enomyenomyenomyenom . . .

Now try saying it up and down:

m
o
n
e
y
m
o
n
e
y
m
o
n
e
y
m
o
n
e
y

What's the point? Exactly. What does money mean? When you look at it like that, it's just a bunch o' letters. Not very pretty letters at that.

Starts to lose its luster after a while. Yet even if we get sick of saying it, we never get sick of *wanting it*.

We want our money. Why? Well, to buy things, right? To get stuff. To pay the bills. We *need* our money.

Do you envy rich people? It's okay; nobody can tell you're reading this right now. If you envy rich people, nod your head. If you're on the subway, people will think you are just another cuckoo, so don't be shy.

I thought so. Me, too. That's right. I already laid my cards on the table in my preface.

"But Ben, this is supposed to be a spiritual book, about finding love and happiness in relationships, and through inner peace."

That it is. I got news for you though. Any fool who thinks that cold hard cash and the acquisition of ladies' love aren't one and the same deserves to be lonely. And don't get me wrong—I really do believe all the goofy theories and ideas on these pages. But would I be offering them just for the "love of writing?" No way, Jose.

And guess what? That's *okay with the universe*.

News flash: The universe embraces honesty!

In fact, I would be willing to go on record saying that almost every author is at this "art thing" for the same reason: greenery. From Salinger on down, they just don't *admit it*.

"Oooh, ooh, I'll never sell the movie rights to

one of my stories." You can bet you won't, J.D. Not with that self-fulfilling prophecy.

I get into this in more detail later, but basically the universe can be looked at as a giant spittoon, accepting all the vile stuff that we hoch up out of our mouths every day. Not a pretty picture, but it's true. Anything that comes out of our mouths, the universe takes as fact, much as your average American tabloid reader in line at the supermarket accepts the *National Enquirer* as law.

Every time we say, "I am just happy to do what I want to do, I don't need to be rich," the *universe hears that*! It has very good ears, by the way. Not only does it hear it, it does that annoying thing the universe has a habit of doing— transforming it into *reality*.

Are you really happy just "doing what you want to do"? Actually think about it. If you had a choice between a) having total creative freedom at the job of your choice and not having any money, or b) being as rich as Midas but you had to . . . oh, I don't know, let's say write another self-help book that nobody needs, which would you choose?

I don't need to tell you my answer.

As long as we tell the universe that we're happy struggling along, it will be happy to oblige. There are enough greedy bastards out there getting it while they can, and the universe is always going to oil the squeaky wheel.

Not that I am endorsing being a "greedy bastard." There are many ways to skin a cat, and the good news is that the universe is not exactly the sharpest pencil in the box.

Just as it takes everything you say quite literally, the flip side of that is true as well. The universe is really quite *naive*. Like the slow cousin you used to have fun with at Christmastime, the universe has no sense of irony.

The question is, how do you make this work for you?

First off, you have to accept several truths that I am about to lay forth that seem to have no grounding in reality. They might sound a little "out there," and I grant you, there is no physical proof for what I am about to tell you. But if you wish to make a lot of money, come along for the ride. Anyone else, you can get off here. Any takers?

Didn't think so. People seem to be incredibly open-minded when it comes to making some mashed potatoes. (By the way, if there are any terms here you might not understand—"pretty prezzys," "mashed potatoes," and so on—just assume they are new, inventive nicknames for money.)

UNIVERSAL LAWS OF MONEY

1. *All Forms of Money Exist on the Ethereal Plane*

Deutschemarks, rubles, yen, dollars, and Euro-dollars are floating right in front of our eyes, in the physical timespace that coexists with our own.

That's right. Money is literally within our grasp—we just can't see it.

"Screw you, Ben," you say. "I'm eating cat food and begging for quarters on Broadway. I can't even pay for a clean pair of underwear, and I sure as hell don't see any dead presidents floating anywhere near my face!"

Fine, you win—if that's an argument that you *want* to win, Rockefeller. Personally, I say it's a sucker's bet.

Why not put as much energy into finding that *ethereal plane* as you do poo-pooing it?

2. *The Universe Wants You to Be Rich and Fat*

The universe is regularly offering opportunities to *manifest money*. The problem is, we're too busy not looking in the right places. Hint: Don't try the bank—unless you've got a mask and a shotgun.

We are constantly missing "signs" the universe

presents to us that practically say "This way to the major moolah, Dumbo."

Have you ever received one of those Publisher's ClearingHouse letters? You know, the ones with friendly Ed McMahon telling you that you may have "already won"?

What do you usually do? If you're like I used to be, you throw it away.

Again, here we are, advertising our need to be destitute to the universe.

Next time Old Beer Breath's sweepstakes shows up on your doorstep, *open it*!! At the very least, you'll get a fine deal on subscriptions to your favorite periodicals. At best, you'll not only become a millionaire beyond your wildest dreams—you'll also become famous!

3. Money Is as Money Does

Money likes money. Ever put two quarters side-by-side? They look kinda happy, don't they? Money likes to be with other money, and it *attracts it*.

How many people do you know who have "penny jars" in their kitchens? Amazing how those babies fill up. It ain't by accident.

Pennies and other forms of currency actually have an electromagnetic attraction to each other.

They have a scientific necessity to be with each

other. While there is no "hard" data to back this up, it is painfully obvious to those of us who ain't got it that the ones who do keep gettin' more! And I, for one, have a hard time believing that all rich people are "financial geniuses."

People who have money are no smarter than you or I, and—here's the joke!—neither is the money it-self. It is very, very simple, and, like the salmon who needs to spawn, the money has only one need—*to be with all the other money*. Starting to get it?

These three laws are inescapable and im-mutable. And by following their basic principles, you can attract all the wealth you might need for the rest of your life.

"So how do I grab all that dough," you ask? Well, let's start with what you got, Mr. or Ms. Getty. As rule number three states, money likes other money.

MAKE A MONEY HOUSE

Money, as I said, has incredible scientific and spiri-tual properties that most of us aren't aware of. The green pigments in American currency have been known to contain traces of chlorophyll, the same chemical found in plants that makes them green. Plants need love, and so does cabbage—dollars, that is. And as everyone who's ever read grandma's throw pillow knows, "Home Is Where the Heart Is." Everybody wants a loving home, and money is no different. As someone who wants a lot of money, you must create a *Loving Monetary Environment*, or LME.

Make a place in your home for money to "live." Your LME doesn't have to be big. Maybe just a little bamboo basket sprinkled with dried garlic or vanilla extract, to make it sweet. Start the party off by leaving a few bucks in there. Hold the bills up to your mouth and tell them, "This is *your* house. Mom and Dad have left for the weekend, and it's party time. Invite all the friends that you want over!"

You'd be surprised how the simple act of just talking to money like a person allows it to blossom into the attractive lure it can be. When you speak to your money, do it in a calm, soothing voice. Speak to it as a lover, flattering it and telling it how beautiful and sexy it is. Make sure you do this alone, as most people will think it's strange. Funny how those same judgmental folks will blow on dice in Vegas and tell them, "Mama needs a new pair of shoes"! I'd prefer to talk directly to my money, thank you much—and take out the middleman.

While the fact that money attracts money can be a good thing, it also accounts for why money is so hard to hold onto. Especially if you are not aware of the natural tendencies of currency. What follows is a typical example:

I have a ten spot and I want to get two fives, so I can leave a tip for the waiter. I give him the ten, he brings me back the two fives, and I leave him one of them for his tip. When I leave that restaurant, I have left both that five *plus* the ten behind. Like it or not, I go home a loser. Why? Because I decided to be a "big man" and show everybody what a good tipper I am. Meanwhile, I'm out five big ones, plus the ten spot I started out with!

The point is, *money slips away, to be with other money.* I can't give you the whys and hows on this. Believe me when I tell you that it rolls through your fingers, especially when you are in a relationship. The money somehow senses this, and like many organisms in nature, finds a way to be with its own.

The "money house" is a sure way to attract money and is a good starting point. You will find varying degrees of success with this method, depending on the climate you are in and the magnetic orientation of the coins and dollars you use. (New currency is always more attractive, especially to older bills.)

Once you have started to learn the properties of money, you can move on to more adventurous and

spiritually challenging quests for cash, which I will
outline in future books dedicated solely to this subject. Until then, go forth with the knowledge that
money, and all things monetary, can actually be
the key to happiness and success both in relationships and your spiritual life. Being poor sucks. Rich
people *are* happier!

JANEANE

(Don't) Listen Up

Most self-help books trumpet the importance of "really" listening to loved ones or coworkers in order for a relationship to thrive. I am here to debunk this theory. You can have your cake and eat it too, if you master the art of "limited income eartake," or LIE. The concept of give-and-take is supposedly important, and being a compassionate listener is perhaps a lovely character trait, but what if you just don't have time to listen?

I don't know if you're aware of this, but it's a jungle out there, and we're pressed for time in here. There are not enough hours in the day for everyone to be attended to.

From the cries of Sinn Fein to the whines of Jackie Mason, everybody's got an agenda and everyone thinks he or she is right. Trying to change someone's mind usually becomes an exercise in futility, so it is your job to pretend to care. Offer some tepid advice and move along. Cultivate the Switzerland[1] in your soul, and remain delightfully detached. (Remember, no agenda or problem is more profound than your own.)

You must reserve your energy and deal with the road bumps in your own life. Concentrate on the self while conning those closest into believing you care about them. (Fortunately, it is possible to abuse and dislike yourself while still pulling focus and ignoring the rantings of others in the room.)

Apply the same channel-surfing or LIE technique when the news gets "too heavy." With remote in hand, give a sympathetic nod and a sigh, then press onward. Big eyes and a slightly tilted head will show loved ones that you empathize with whatever the hell they're saying now. This display of friendship will encourage your partner to think well of you. When partner thinks well of you, you can extract favors and items from partner.[2]

What others think of your presentation is the *most* important thing, so whatever it takes to manipulate the man/woman in your life into believing

---

1. Offering to *hold on to* people's jewelry and art is another option.

2. Again, adopt the Swiss idea of conveniently forgetting where the jewelry and art you were holding is.

in you is what you'll do. (Employees and relatives should also learn to say "how high" once you've said "jump.") I don't know whether to quote Malcolm or Machiavelli here, but you get the gist.

A lovely paradigm for feigned compassion is the American politician. Carefully monitor the body language and demeanor of your garden-variety senator. The "senatorial gaze," as we shall call it henceforth, is one of indifference wrapped in a candy shell of receptiveness. I can't even look at bunting[3] without pretending to care about something.

Learn from those guys behind the podium. They have no desire to meet you halfway, and history tells us that there's no need to. Walking a mile in another man's *zapatos* is a lovely gesture, but hardly necessary. As you argue with your mate, conjure images of Newtie, Helmsie, and Strommie. Who better to teach the ways of the supremely selfish, a.k.a. "the rugged individualist"?

Your anvil, stirrup, and hammer can only take so much vibration.[4] These are the three most delicate bones in your body. Limit the abuse they take and listen selectively. If the man/woman in your life doesn't "play ball," aurally bench them. I cannot

---

3. Bunting is a twofold source of pain for me. See "Intermission Statement: A Denial of Self-Indulgence."

4. Those three tiny bones have suffered enough. See the chapter "How to Build a Relationship on Next to Nothing."

emphasize enough how important it is to devote the majority of your time and brain juice to yourself.

Even if it's irrational, repetitive and potentially harmful, as an author my main concern is that you become convinced that too much contemplation is still not enough.[5] You can never read enough books about your own needs. *Your* needs are paramount. Cost should be of no concern in your pursuit to pay more attention to yourself, while perfecting the art of seeming to care for others. Turn inward, and cash will be thrown outward. Reach toward others so that they will give unto you.

As pertains to a loving, healthy relationship, I suggest you seek out a man/woman whose dysfunction dovetails with your own id-meets-ego tendencies. Two people with a strong sense of entitlement do not meld harmoniously.[6] Find the runt in the litter and build from there.[7]

---

5. Narcissistic, neurotic behavior deserves another mention, as it is the prime mover behind the highly lucrative self-help, New Age, fitness, psychoanalytic, and hair care industries.

6. Sex is the exception to this rule. There is no harm in sleeping with someone completely ill-suited and downright surly. Basing a one-night stand on lust and mutual disgust can lead to a very fulfilling four hours. It's okay to expect the least.

7. In my next book I'll tell you how to arrange your furniture according to the tenets of Feng Shui, thereby maximizing your ability to enjoy a "one-night stand" or "abbreviated encounter."

BEN

Road Diary

So, you wanna write a self-help book. You sit down and start to sift through all the little tidbits of advice, rules, theories, and ideas that you have gathered in that musty old attic you call a brain. You realize that as a man at the end of the twentieth century who lives in a major city and has a general knowledge of current events and pop culture, who watches a lot of TV, and who has no real religious ties, you are awash in a culture filled with media gurus who will offer you everything from seven ways to become highly "effective" to seven ways to "heal your life" to seven bowls of chicken soup for your soul. The whole damn subject has been covered seven ways to Sunday. So what do you do?

You run away.

At least that's what I did. I realized that the only way I would be able to clear my mind of all that mumbo jumbo out there and get in touch with my true inner being—that scared little ragamuffin who wants nothing more than to skip around in a muumuu and throw rose petals at the sun—was to shirk all my everyday responsibilities and go on the road.

And that's what I did—armed with nothing but a healthy per diem from the publisher, a cellular phone with full roaming capabilities, and one of those cool new backpacks, courtesy of the good people at Jansen.

No hotel rooms, no amenities—just camping out and living like a gypsy—nothing to get between me and myself except my own fears. I set out for a one-year adventure of the soul.

My goal was to travel as much of this country as I could in one year. Not using air travel at all, I was determined to hike and hitch the highways and byways and make my destinations the little, off-the-beaten-track nowheresvilles. I thought that if I ventured far from civilization as I knew it— places where nonfat mochas are just a thing you read about in *USA Today*—but still had the per diem in case I needed to get the hell out if I was going *too* crazy, then I might truly be able to clean the slate, as it were, and figure out what I had to say.

It ended up turning out really badly, but the lessons I learned were invaluable. There are some wonderful folk out there in this land we call America, and there are also some scary freaks.

But the point was to experience the good with the bad, and that I did.

I got some mighty soul learning, and I wouldn't trade any of it. Not for nothin'.

DAY 1: LOS ANGELES

Today is Day One. I get up at 5:45 and drag my weary bones into the shower—the last hot one I'll be taking for quite some time, probably. The previous night, I packed my rucksack and made all the appropriate goodbyes, explaining to my friends and loved ones that I was going on a one-year journey of the soul and that they shouldn't be surprised if they don't hear from me for a long spell.

By 10 A.M., I am at the entrance to Interstate 10, headed east, my thumb out and my heart open. There are no takers for a long time. After about two hours, a highway patrolman pulls over. He is blond, with a brush cut and tinted orange aviators. He asks me what I am doing. I tell him that by hook or by crook, I am going to get in touch with myself—that I am on a "visionquest," if you will. He threatens to arrest me, telling me it is illegal to hitchhike on an interstate.

Interesting thing about policemen. It seems they always like to tell you what to do.

He tells me to get my "ass off the highway" before he "kicks it off for me." I look him in the eyes, realizing how hard it must be to do his job, every day having to tell people what to do, where to go. Seeing death, crime, and all sorts of bad stuff.

I bet nobody hardly ever looks him in the eyes and sees beyond the badge. Experiment time.

Maybe the simple idea of just *talking to him, like a regular joe*, might open him up.

"It's a hot one, ain't it, Officer . . . Hancock. I bet you're all sweaty in that tight get-up."

"Shut the fuck up and get facedown on the ground, now!"

Funny how sometimes when you try something and it doesn't work, you don't get the message—you keep making the same mistake. I think that I can somehow "change" Officer H. Maybe teach him about communication.

"Don't you think it's kinda silly, two grown men standing by a highway, one of them all dressed up in a blue—"

My speech is interrupted by a blow to my jaw from his nightstick, the blood from my dislodged tooth flying onto the shoulder of my T-shirt. It is very clear that Officer Hancock will be doing the teaching today.

I am taken to the Rampart division, where I am booked and charged. Too embarrassed to call anyone, I spend my first night on the road in lockup with a couple of young, jonesing crackheads who don't seem too keen on learning to open up, either.

And it is perfect.

The next morning the judge lets me go after I

explain that I am writing a book and this was all part of my spiritual journey. He seems impressed, having read *A Course in Miracles*.

He wishes me luck on the road, advising me to stay off the main arteries.

Kinda interesting, the judge being the least "judgmental."

Hmm. It's going to be quite a year.

DAY 6: SOMEWHERE IN THE DESERT OUTSIDE VICTORVILLE

Six days from home and it feels like a year already. The only thing that reminds me it's been less than a week is the space where my left upper incisor used to be and an infected gum where Officer Hancock's "lesson" didn't heal right.

Since then I've been hitching and walking, mainly the latter. I don't know about a year. That seems like an awfully long time, and I have already learned a lot about myself. Like how goddamned sunburned I can get spending twelve hours a day on the road.

Jesus, I miss TV.

I think I'll go to Vegas. I bet I can learn a lot about myself there.

Yeah. That sounds good. Anywhere with some goddamned AC.

DAY 7: VEGAS

What a difference a junior suite makes! I'm already feeling much better about the whole situation. I think I just needed a good meal and a soft bed for a night. Tomorrow I'll light out again into this great country of ours, ready to find some answers.

But tonight, a few games of chance are in order!

DAY 8: VEGAS

Played the wheel all night. The bastard wheel. I guess there are some really great metaphors about roulette and the soul. Like how if you place all the "money" of your soul on 14, your soul can really get "fucked."

Maybe this is a lesson I need to learn, something about focusing on wanting one thing, but the universe enlightening me by not giving it to me.

One thing's for sure, the beautiful sun will rise in about two hours, meaning I'll be able to get another three hundred from the cash machine. I'd hate to leave here down.

DAYS 9–12: VEGAS

Still down.

DAY 13: BROKEN BACK, NEVADA

Having finally had some luck at the craps table, I decide to celebrate with a trip out to one of Nevada's famed "ranches."

At the small permanent trailer site, I am introduced to Amber. She is about 5'3", blonde and perky, though with a very husky voice. I tell her this is my first time with a prostitute where it is actually legal.

She is kind and gentle with me, lightly stroking my ass, which even though it is kind and gentle, freaks me out. I ask her if it's okay if we just talk. She tells me sure, that lots of her customers just like to talk.

I tell her I am on a one-year journey of the soul, trying to break free of all my prestructured ways of looking at things, in hopes of getting to the core of who I am or, as I call it, REALME.

She quickly ushers me back into the waiting area and talks to an older, leather-skinned woman. After about a minute, a much larger black lady who introduces herself as Roxette tells me she will be my date now.

I ask her if we can just talk this time, not explaining what I am up to. Very quickly I realize we have little in common. Between the long, uncomfortable silences, she tells me she is the mother of three and is taking two courses in Communications at Ely Community College.

I would have never guessed it. Some books can't be read by their covers, can they?

As she shares her own very mundane story with me I realize that, without even being aware, I have put her in a category as "hooker," when in reality she is a "person" who *happens* to be a "hooker." And a pretty accomplished hooker at that. Her GPA is 3.5!

I guess when we stop putting people into little boxes, or cubbyholes, we can finally stop expecting them to act like they're in kindergarten.

And what Roxette did to me next had nothing to do with kindergarten—let me assure you.

DAY 14: SOMEWHERE OVER ARKANSAS

I finally wise up and realize that if I stay with this whole "travel by byway" thing I will be in the desert for like three more months. The whole point of this trip was to see a lot of different environments, meet a lot of different people. I think I've met enough people from California and Nevada.

So I obtain an open ticket on American Airlines. The great thing about the good people at American is that besides being friendly, courteous, and hard-working, they also seem to appreciate what it means to be seen as an airline that caters to a young, hip demographic. Just good folks.

As I look out the window, the great plains of the middle west stretch out below me like lazy pan-cakes on a simmering griddle. A thunderstorm to the south pours like syrup onto the brown fields.

I wonder if they serve breakfast on this flight. In first class, you would think they would.

DAY 16: PONCA CITY, OKLAHOMA

Sometimes you can learn about life from the unlikeliest teachers.

Today I found myself face to face with one such teacher. His breath smelled like hell and his hair was falling out in patches. He defecated in front of me and then tried to bite me. No, no, I'm not talking about some crazy rock 'n' roll punker (though I have heard of some of them acting like that). I *am* talking about Popo.

Popo is a Mexican Chihuahua who joined me in the back of my pickup ride somewhere around Joplin. I can't tell you the exact hour, but we were both unceremoniously dumped on the Ponca City exit sometime around dawn. Having no recollection of the previous night's events, but feeling the aftereffects of something that caused my lower abs to be uncommonly sore, I sat by the roadway and contemplated my new friend. Where had he come from? Where had I come from, for that matter? The question didn't seem to interest Popo in the least. He seemed to have a much more immediate concern: Licking the smile off my face!

Now, I grew up in a big city, where "dogs" were what you called your feet when they were tired, or what you ate off steaming buns in Central Park. I had never been privy to the beautiful, simple *un-*

conditional love of a canine. Well, from the second I came to in the back of that pickup, Popo layering me with doggie saliva that was as putrid-smelling as the worst rotten eggs, yet as loving as an embrace from the Pope (thus the inspiration for his name—"little pope" in Spanish), I was hooked.

We spent a few days together, traveling through the middle of Oklahoma. On those long nights that I intentionally spent in the cheapest motels I could find, Popo revealed to me what is most definitely a sacred world: The Secret Life of Dog Lovers. And its main event: the nighttime cuddle. Now I get it!

Just ask the Boss; he said it best: "Ain't nobody like to sleep alone . . ." And when you have a dog, you have what every human craves—something to rub up against in the middle of the night. Popo is a small little mite, but I imagine the bigger in size, well . . . I believe it was David St. Hubbins who penned the lyric "The bigger the cushion, the sweeter the pushin'."

Now, before you go off and call the NAACP, or whatever, try to understand me. I am not in any way condoning bestiality.

The point I make, and any honest-with-themselves dog owner will own up to this, is that there is a certain . . . license, if you will, that one can take with the canine cuddlemate. Let's face it—Snoop Doggy Dogg has got it right when he croons about the Doggystyle.

The point is, "snuggling" is "snuggling." With human, ferret, wildebeest, or Martian!

How refreshing I found it to be able to rub up against something in the middle of the night whose first reaction wasn't to scream about sexual harassment or to just plain turn its back on me. I'm sure I am striking a chord with many of you here. When's the last time a dog complained about "molestation"?

No, they live and love. Yes, sometimes that pink turkey popper indicator thing comes out when you believe the experience is purely platonic, but before we point the finger at the poor pooch, let's remember that for every overexcited canine, there is the lonely housewife who has nothing but a jar of Skippy and a come-hither look for Fido. Now I ain't sayin *where* that Skippy's goin', but let's just say it's not between a couple of slices of Wonder Bread White.

What the dog represents is our true, wonderful animal nature. We can connect with them because they are at once animal (wild, crazy, and all those other adjectives that people use when describing animals) and they are also domesticated. In other words, we can have our id and eat it too.

Now I don't want to get too technical here.

Animal psychology was not one of the courses I studied during my brief tenure at the University of California at Los Angeles. (No, there I studied Partying 101, my friend—for which I graduated magna cum *lawdy*!) But that is a whole 'nother can o' gravy.

The domestic nature of our four-legged barking companions makes them less threatening to us, thus allowing us to spend much time in close proximity to them. (You wouldn't invite a Somalian hyena to hop up in bed with you to watch Nick at Nite.) We trust them. Most of the time, they don't hurt us. In fact, we tend to see them as elaborate toys, or in some cases actually use them as substitutes for real people.

For me, people never got realer than Popo. But alas, he is no more. We parted company just outside of some town near some other town in Oklahoma. I forgot to feed him, and he seemed to lose interest in me rather quickly, growing wan and melancholy and finally refusing to move altogether. But I will always remember the simple life lesson that the little Chihuahua from 'round Joplin way taught me—a lesson that sadly he himself could never learn: Believe in the true nature of all things, and you will forever live in the glory of absolute forgiveness.

Ruff ruff, little pope. I miss ya.

DAY 22: PORT PICKNEY, TEXAS

Three things you learn pretty quick about the town of Port Pickney. One, there's no water for five hundred miles in any direction. The "Port" was a misprint on the municipal charter back in 1873—it was actually a "Fort" in the Civil War.

Two, if you were born there you're called a "Port Pickner"—an honor bestowed upon the majority of the town's 243 residents.

And three, they love their Ring Toss.

On a day trip out of Dallas, I come across PP, as locals refer to it, about two hours south of the city. There's no exit—so don't bother searchin' for it. You get off at the sign for Waco, and then you get lost for about an hour and it's right there on the left.

My rented Lexus is sucking fumes as I lurch into Port Pickney Pump 'n' Pay. As the kindly old codger fills my tank, his C.A.T. baseball cap slightly askew on a forehead that has seen its share of sweat drops, I ask him what a fella looking for fun and spiritual enlightenment could find around town.

He takes about two minutes—a real two minutes, which is a long time—and doesn't say anything, just points across the street. I later learned he was a deaf-mute.

Across the Road is a rusty red-and-white wooden sign reading "Pickney Ring Rodeo." After paying the codger, I amble across the street for a gander.

Well, I must have shown up on a special day, because it seems like two-thirds of the Port Pickners are gathered around what looks like an old horse corral, watching a heavyset woman with black braids "toss ring."

She stands about thirty feet from an iron spike that pokes out of the dirt. Crouched in a surfer-type stance, Mama Whitefeather, as I would soon learn was her name, tosses five rings in a row at the spike, nailing it with deadly accuracy. Each time she hits, the crowd of locals whoop and holler.

When she finishes, she holds her thick and gelatinous arms over her head, "Rocky" style, exciting the crowd even more. Almost shamanlike, this Ring Toss Tillie is clearly the town's spiritual warrior queen.

I buy her a hearty lunch at the Pickney Po' Boy's, and she shares some of her life philosophy with me, in between mouthfuls of some of the sloppiest pork barbecue this city boy has ever seen.

"Ring toss is life; life is ring toss," she exhales.

Life is ring toss. You got that one right, Mama. I think back on the last few years of my hectic life.

I've been "tossing rings"—running around in circles, trying to reach goals in my career, relationships, and social life that never seem to come together. The problem is, my rings always seem to come up short of that darned spike.

"What do you think about when you toss the rings?"

Mama Whitefeather, a half-Sioux, half-Greek bachelorette, doesn't look up as she continues scooping the spicy meat into her mouth.

"I think about tossing rings. Just like when I eat barbecue, I think about eating barbecue."

And boy, can she eat. Yes, when you toss the ring, *toss the ring*. When you eat barbecue, *really eat it*.

"But don't you ever get overwhelmed or frustrated? Aren't there days when the rings just don't hit the spike?"

At this point she belches a long, satisfying pork belch, the kind that comes only after *really eating*. She looks me in the eyes for the first time, as if I am a very slow child.

"Ring toss is life; life is ring toss."

Wouldn't it be wonderful if we could all share her simplicity of purpose, her uncomplicated, Gump-like view of things?

Maybe "Ring toss is life; life is ring toss,"

should be our rallying cry in this crazy, mixed-up carnival of a world. Toss rings; ask questions later.

She finishes the last of her food, literally licking her plate as she gets up from the table.

Before she leaves, I ask her if she might give me some directions to get back to the city.

Curiously, her simple philosophy of life doesn't translate to her navigational skills. She gives me the most unclear and obfuscating set of instructions to get to the interstate, repeatedly describing in detail landmarks that if I saw them would mean I had gone too far (one of my pet peeves).

As Port Pickney recedes in my rear view, I catch a glimpse of Mama returning to her corral and her beloved rings, a woman whose view of the world is so damn narrow that Kate Moss would have trouble fitting in.

DAY 23: ASPEN, COLORADO

Things have taken a turn for the worse. I flew in about an hour ago. In attempting to check in at the Ritz Carlton, my card is declined. It turns out my damn Vegas expenses are catching up with me.

I think the combined stress of not being near New York or Los Angeles for almost a month—and not having checked my machine for over three weeks—is finally getting to me.

DAY 24

I'm Ben fucking Stiller, you would think they would at least let me sleep on the goddamned couch in their stupid lobby. I hate Aspen.

DAY 25: MOTEL SIX, CRESTED CRACK, COLORADO

I feel as if I am on the moon.

I guess the moon isn't the worst place to be if you like cheese. Or maybe the key is to be a mouse. What the hell does that mean? I don't know. I think I'm freaking out.

DAY 26

Well, I spent the last twenty bucks I had on this beautiful one-room shithole.

I can hear people doing it in the next room. How pleasant.

Funny thing about people in motels. They always seem to . . . oh fuck it.

DAY 27: STREET OUTSIDE MOTEL SIX

Cold. So cold.

I wanna go home now.

DAY 28

My dad comes and picks me up. He flies in from New York. He doesn't look very proud of me. He gives me the same look he gave me when he picked me up from baseball camp after two days when I was twelve.

Thank God this is over.

JANEANE

The Ugly Truth

From the man on the street to the cop on the beat, we can all agree that it is better to be attractive. Your mother lied; looks are everything, and the sooner you submit and stop denying the inevitable, the happier you will be.

Do not misunderstand me. I dislike attractive people, as they are usually silly and weak, but it is in your best interest to try and curry their favor. You reap the benefits if there is a gorgeous guy/girl in your immediate social set. Broken-down vehicles and meager funds at a bar are easily rectified if your easy-on-the-eyes mate seeks the kindness of strangers. It is not wrong to hitch your wagon to someone else's face. Surely they won't notice your parasitic behavior since eight out of ten homecoming kings/queens are utterly dull witted.

In fact, just staring into the eyes of a model or actress can cause one to sleep uncontrollably. They lack the initial fortitude that semesters of being treated like Barakumin[1] on campus can build. Year after year, brick by brick, a character built on the foundation of shopping in the Sears husky section and remote corners of the junior miss/mister shops gives you the right to look back in anger and forward in condescension.

It is a feeling akin to the sphincter-tightening sensation provoked by the statement: "Cindy Crawford is considered a larger, voluptuous model." Journalists know not what they do. It is unfortunate that pretty people misunderstand the sheer triteness of their existence. Society rewards them for unintentional genetic blessings, and we are then left holding the chagrin bag. Lovely ones don't grasp that succeeding and being lovely is an easy task, the road most traveled, if you will. (Will you?) It is a far greater challenge to succeed and

---

1. A lower-level inhabitant in the Hindu caste system. Barakumin, ethnically indistinguishable from other Japanese, are descendants of those who had occupations considered to be "unclean," like skinning animals or burying the dead. For a traditional Hindu of the upper castes, untouchables (lower castes) pollute everything they come into contact with. Most live their lives in terrible poverty and humiliation. The Hindu religion assigns superiority and inferiority on the basis of birth.

Please replace the word *birth* with *physical appeal*, and you will understand the American way.

have people rave about what a great set of "cerebral lobes" you have.

No one is surprised when *le petit fleuris* company is highly coveted at any and every soirée, a woeful tradition that started with the Big Bang, when the most attractive amoeba slithered from the primordial soup and went on to become the most popular biped. Same story, different post-Cambrian era. As Americans—nay, as Earth dwellers—we embrace beauty in all its mediocrity. From the Ubangi lip plate to the silicone boob, all societies capitalize on this theme.

Entertainment, in particular, is a machine that fuels itself on the faces and bodies of its bland participants. (Again, it is not wrong for you to resent and harbor irrational venom toward VJs, soap stars, and box-office draws.) Most participants in the popular arts have earned their stripes the good ol' fashioned way: by being better looking than you or your parents. I call this phenomenon the Burns/Bahns insult.[2] Let the queen's rebuke to Cardinal Wolsey capture the sentiment: "I do believe, induced by potent circumstances, that thou art mine enemy."

Surely, my "potent circumstances" are less noble than the queen's, given her situation, but they

---

2. Rent *The Brothers McMullen*.

haunt me nonetheless. My point being, dear reader, it is perfectly normal, healthy, and right-minded to heap ill will upon those more fortunate and attractive.

Maslow warned of the difficulty in reaching the top of his hierarchy. If self-actualization is out of our grasp, then why not emit insecurities like an errant lawn sprinkler?

Liberation from cumbersome ideals and glad tidings leaves one free to use sarcastic barbs and derisive statements. It's a cosmic system of checks and balances kept harmonious by your decision to loathe the attractive for no good reason.

PUKING FASTER-MATION©

As I lovingly expurgate all the contents of my stomach,
so do I expunge all bad thoughts and contrary messages.
As I wretch and heave, violently purging my alcohol-
    poisoned vessel,
so do I purge all belief-system untruths that I have
    wrongly followed in my liquor-induced haze.
I remember that this feeling of nausea and sickness will
    soon pass,
just as I remind myself that next time I will drink more
    water before going to sleep.
And as I wipe the putrid spittle from my dry and brittle
    lips, I rejoice in the perfect knowledge
that all is well in the world, and now I will be able to
    sleep it off.

BEN

Selfhood

"I ain't no Little Red Riding Hood!"
(He fires his tommy gun into Dutch Schultz.)
—Lucky Luciano, as portrayed by Andy Garcia
in the motion picture *HOODLUM*
(cut from the "R" version)

It seems to me we're all hung up on "hoods": Parenthood. Couplehood. Babyhood. The list can go on and on, and many people wish it didn't—just ask Patrick "Father Hood" Swayze.

Hood seems to be an all-encompassing term for a lot of nothing. What does it mean in the search for happiness and fulfillment in your own life? When we sat down to write this, we considered titling the book *FEELTHISBOOKHOOD*—if for no other reason than people might mistakenly believe this was another Paul Reiser bestseller.

People love to label things in this country, and the *hood* suffix seems to be the label du jour. But all the labels in the world won't bring you any closer to true happiness, either alone or in a relationship. I know, 'cause I've been there and back. Let's talk about Depressionhood or Sexual Addictionhood—yeah, or how about a little Suicidaltendencyhood—you don't see Opie Griffith lining up to make a movie about that one, do ya? If you're anything like me on a bad day, these are all real problems that we have to deal with on a daily basis. And all the Zoloft in the world can't change the worst one of all, "I don't like *me* hood."

Call it what you want, but these feelings of self-loathing affect a lot of us, even the toughest homeys (call that *Boyz N the Hood*–hood).

If we are to cast away these deeply embedded feelings of inferiority, we must invent new "hoods" that label the true potentiality that we can embody.

Perhaps the best way to do this is by making these images real for ourselves. People can tell you how hot the stove is till they're blue in the face, but only by searing your flesh on a scorching burner will you understand the true meaning of their warning. In much the same way, I can write all day about how you should "change your attitude" or "find a new perspective" on your life, but until you have been "seared" by my message in a concrete way, it will remain merely words on a page. Now don't worry—I won't burn you. But I sure hope I make you a little hot under the collar, 'cause that means I'm rockin' your boat.

So let's talk hoods. Real, honest to goodness hoods. Get some pillowcases and cut some eyes out. I would advise staying away from the white ones.

Buy about ten of them—you're going to wear them a lot. Now get a marker—one of those indelible jobs. You want the message to be loud and clear and not fade away.

Take the first hood. Write out the letters "M-A-D" under your eyeholes. This will be your MADHOOD. Part of this therapy is about identifying how you are feeling about yourself and accepting it. When you get angry, instead of holding it in, you will put on your MADHOOD. That way you don't have to say anything to anybody—because it's written all over your face. Literally.

Make a SADHOOD, an ENVYHOOD, a HUN-GRYHOOD, a LONELYHOOD, a HORNYHOOD, a POUTYHOOD, a HURTHOOD, a CHEERFULHOOD, and a BORINGHOOD.

Carry each of these in a pouch, or HOODSACK,

that you keep with you at all times. When you feel a mood swing coming on, whip out the appropriate hood and put it on. Immediately you will be telling your partner and the world "where you're at" emotionally. And you won't have to make up silly excuses for why you're behaving the way you are.

Just imagine how much simpler it will make a night with your girlfriend! Say she wants to go see a movie at the local art house, but you'd rather see the newest Van Damme offering. She's all hung up on seeing some documentary about Russian coal miners. As usual, you suppress your true anger and decide to go along. In the car, about halfway to the movie theater, she turns to you and says that she knows you're angry about going. You deny it. There is a long silence.

You buy your Jujubes at the movie house and sit through the wretched black-and-white snooze-inducer, wishing you were eating a pizza instead. You both go home silently, and when it comes time for a little good-night lovin', you're left high and dry. Feeling rejected, you pick a fight about nothing. You end up sleeping on the couch. When you wake in the morning, both of you feel bad about the fight, and you kiss and make up. But you go to work wondering why you had to go through all that in the first place.

Now, imagine if you had the HOODSACK. When your girlfriend first suggests the idea of the Russian documentary, you can immediately put on your BORINGHOOD. This will tell her right off the bat that you aren't too thrilled with the idea of being two hundred feet below the Ukrainian bedrock for the next 120 minutes. If she still insists on going, in the car on the way to the theater you can reach into your pouch and put on the POUTY-HOOD. There it is right in front of her, no confusion. She won't even ask if you are pouting, 'cause it's *written right across your face.*

Now, if by this time she isn't getting the message (and by the way, if she has *her* HOODSACK, she can respond—i.e., placing her MADHOOD on in response to your POUTYHOOD), once you are in the theater, you will slap on the HUNGRYHOOD. That way, when your girlfriend glances your way, she will know what you need—and the patrons at the theater won't be bothered by her having to ask if you are okay. You can then go to get your pizza, and return in time to take her home.

Once in bed you'll slip on your HORNYHOOD. Hopefully, she will put hers on as well. Guys, if she puts on the BORINGHOOD, you're in trouble! In the morning, you'll both slip on your CHEERFUL-HOODS, because everybody has expressed their feelings.

TIPS ON HOODS

The hood method is one that works. However, in adopting it, as in any new form of self-help therapy, you need to be aware of certain pitfalls.

1. It Takes Time

Getting used to wearing a hood isn't easy. You might want to cut out a mouth hole in your HUNGRYHOOD. You'll find that when you wear it you get results damn quick, and the hood tends to attract food particles to it quite easily. This can make for a SMELLYHOOD if you're not diligent about washing it.

Also, in addition to mouth holes, you might want to make ear holes, too. I have found this especially helpful in couples who are both using hoods. Though you are both being up-front about your feelings, if you have a hood over your head it is hard to hear what the other person is verbally expressing to you.

2. Have a Thick Skin

People will make fun of you at first for wearing a hood on your head. Coworkers, loved ones, even your children are likely to be put off, initially. There is really nothing you can do about this, save for wearing your HURTHOOD when they ridicule you. Also, as I said before, avoid the white hoods. From a distance, people will not be able to read the writing on the front, and they might get the wrong idea. If you do have to wear a white hood, make sure you make up an extra one for your pouch that reads "NOTKKKHOOD" in bold letters.

3. You Gotta Be in It to Win It!

Stick with it. It ain't easy to start opening up your true soul to the world, even if by doing it with a hood you are also anonymous (one of the perks for shy people).

When I see a fellow HOODSACK toter comin' at me down the street, I feel that tingle in my soulbelly that comes from the pride of knowing that there are folks out there who are trying to change their lives. I tip my sack to each and every one of them. As you put on your various hoods throughout your day, be strong in the knowledge that you are not alone.

Hood-ray for you!

Advanced Hoods

For those of you who feel comfortable in your HOODSACK mode, you are ready to take it to the next step. Each of these hoods represent "bigger"

truths that you may or may not wish to reveal.
Make sure that you wear these Level 2 hoods only
around *other HOODSACKERS*. Also, rubber might be
better than pillowcase for these hoods, for obvious
reasons.

GAYHOOD

I strongly urge using this as a "coming out"
method. What better way to announce your pride
in your sexuality than by wearing it plastered to
your face! Again, for those of you concerned with
not letting certain people know, the anonymity
factor works for you here.

TOURETTESHOOD

Again, a perfect "icebreaker" for sufferers of this
upsetting affliction. This way your boss will see
it coming when you call him a "cocksucking
motherfucker!"

MICHAELBOLTONFANHOOD

You people owe it to the rest of us to put your
cards on the table right from the start. Just so we
know who we're dealing with.

CRACKHEADHOOD

Best to go with a fire retardant material on these.

IT'SABEAUTIFULDAYINTHENEIGHBORHOOD
This would be worn to let people know that you are really Mr. Fred T. Rogers. Kind of an obscure one, but ultimately revealing if you are, indeed, Mister Rogers.

JANEANE

Nice, Schmice

Many people feel that mass acceptance and smooth socialization are desirable life paths for a young adult.

Many people are often wrong.

Don't bother being nice. Being popular and well liked is not in your best interest. Let me be more clear; if you behave in a manner pleasing to most, then you are probably doing something wrong. The masses have never been arbiters of the sublime, and they often fail to recognize the truly great individual.[1] Taking into account the public's regrettable lack of taste, it is incumbent upon you not to fit in.

Every time a wedding reception cheers a deejay's choice of "Shout" or "Neutron Dance" you

---

1. Please read *The Crowd* by Gustav Lebon to illustrate this point. He is a better writer than me (or is it "than I"?).

are required to severely clog the toilet in the Hyatt. This type of leftist karma fortifies your "light spirit"[2] and enables you to sneer your way through all family and corporate functions. Not only is the "I" missing from "Team," the "joy" is, too. The "leftist light spirit" inhabits all who embrace the notion of righteous indignation and drink too much around those who frown upon it.

I do not mean to paint a picture of myself as superior or to align myself with genius of any kind. But I am confident in my ability to spot a backward-baseball-capped fraternity brother and then place the appropriate size of chip on my shoulder. Carrying a shoulder chip is like a siren's call to your leftist light spirit who will no doubt share in your contempt for said Greek and inspire you to shun all things the college boy holds dear. Avoid his tastes in music, programming, and peers, and you should be able to fashion a nice life for you and your kin.

Some might say a more Christian attitude of "live and let live" might be healthier for the soul. It is unso. Organized religions and their dogmas only serve to indoctrinate the participants into

---

2. The light spirit is not to be confused with Vox Number One. The spirit is more like a feeling or sensation. These "feelsations" manifest themselves sensorially, not aurally like a voice or voices inside your (or in this case *my*) head. Feelsations have the ability to move you, but they are not bossy, like headvox or roommates.

sheeplike common behaviors. This type of blind assimilation promotes the popularity of top-forty radio stations and movie sequels. Train your light spirit to shun God.[3]

Skepticism toward groups, holy or otherwise, is enriching and makes you a far more entertaining drinking companion. When was the last time a deeply religious or optimistic person caused you to laugh heartily (for the right reasons)? I rest my case.

---

3. Having said that, let me put forth a disclaimer, reminiscent of Pascal's wager, to cover the small of my back with the Divine One:

Dear God, Allah, Yahweh, Japanese Corporation, Buddha, Jehovah, Lama, or Whomever Reigns Supreme. Please forgive me for doubting your existence and deliver me unto the grand hereafter, if in fact there is such a place because I don't want to be left out if everyone else gets to go. (Being cynical throughout eternity is counterproductive.)

MASTURBATION FASTER-MATION©

*With a firm and loving hand I whack away, and in so
 doing I whack away all old patterns of self-hatred,
 replacing them with self-love and caring.*

As I furiously jerk myself into a frenzy,
forgetting all but the task at hand,
*I am at one with the universe that centers around my-
 self.*

*As I focus love and good thoughts into the palm of my
 hand, I repeat over and over*
Me me me! Me me me!

*And as I release my load out into the cosmos, I release
 the past and all of its baggage, relaxing in the perfect knowledge that I am a loving and responsive
 partner to myself and I in no way have to worry
 about getting myself to leave before morning without
 it being awkward.*

JANEANE

Clean and Jerk This

bundant lip service is paid to the theory of a mind-body connection. The concept being that a healthy body begets a highly effective mind, which leads to self-actualization[1] and the building of a better tomorrow.

In regard to fitness equaling brain power, the people you meet in gyms blow that theory just by existing. Listen to any locker room conversation and you'll discover a regrettable lack of mental "effectiveness."[2]

Homo sapiens did not labor to walk upright only to damage their spines in step class. There is

---

1. Mazlow said that most people will never achieve self-actualization, so don't bother trying. A reference so nice we'll use it twice!

2. Studies show that gang-showering reduces intelligence.

no need to lunge and leap about in a room where the music drones but the air is funky. It's an embarrassment of riches as far as mirrors are concerned, and this abundance implies vanity. Vanity leads to hubris, and hubris felled many a Greek. (I do not mean the campus variety.) Back in the day, the cure for hubris might have been a crow picking at your liver or perhaps your eternally rolling a rock up a hill. Modern times gives us a trip to the gynecologist or a colonic. And going to the gym exacerbates tendencies toward hubris that may be lying dormant.

Sightings of butt thongs and mesh half shirts are evidence of this alarming behavior. The thong is a provocative piece of clothing,[3] and I don't mean that in the erotic way. I mean provocative as in provoked, as in provoking me to lash out and cause grievous bodily harm. This disturbing display of vanity had its origins with Vaslav Nijinsky. In 1911, Nijinsky opted not to wear the requisite floppy shorts while dancing Giselle. The audience was aghast at seeing a stranger's "buttocks" and "cod piece."

The brain becomes clouded as eyes see red. The best way to thwart this type of ocular offense is to avoid all gyms and pool parties. The latter are rife

---

3. See Ken Starr report.

with hubris, pure and simple; being too big for one's britches (or in this case, Speedo) is a crime against democracy. It undercuts my freedom *not* to look at your ass region. My rights as a free-sighted individual are rendered as obsolete as the thorough-bred Derby champ gone to glue.

Some would accuse me of bitterness borne from feelings of inadequacy. Some would be wrong indeed. I know a valid windmill when I see one. The health nut is a worthy jousting opponent.

As Americans, we should avoid exercise because it limits our ability to enjoy sloth or slothfulness.[4] Dante would not have devoted a ring to it if it wasn't vital. Slothlike individuals know how to live right. They understand the benefit of sleeping to kill time or sitting to avoid motion. Exercise fosters unhealthy ideas about small, clingy shirts and low-slung jeans. Constricting clothing limits oxygen flow to the brain, thereby reducing personality capacity among the physically fit. The sins of pride are usually located near the Stairmaster. So stay pure and sit down.

---

4. I believe that my decision to remain unfit at the age of thirty-four will serve me well in the future, as I never have to endure the hushed observation that I've really "let myself go."

BEN

Angels in the Outhouse

"Lo, for I have been lifted to the heavens
by the stark white light of unrepentant sinners,
And they will forever bask in the glory of *The
Neverending Story!* And faeries and munchkins will
dance and delight to sweet honeywine music of
the Lord's winged do-gooders—just christen me
the Angel of the Morning!"

    —Twelfth-century incantation

What I write here I write without irony or sarcasm. I know that I am taking a chance, this book being considered "humorous," but as I stated in my introduction, this journey has taken me far and wide of such a low objective.

I feel that any book seeking to open up to the

reader areas of self-growth must be wholeheartedly and unabashedly raw. What I lay before you is a lovingly told tale, straight from my heart. No advice or "how-to" in this chapter—just an honest account of a little old event that changed my life forever.

I never used to believe in angels. You know, cute little cherubic winged Botticelli babies and the like. I put them right up there with Santy Claus and the Tooth Fairy. Wonderful dreams for a child to have, but like all childhood fantasies, at a certain age the myth must be crushed and we all are forced to grow up and deal with life's harsh realities.

I had certain "enlightened" friends who told me otherwise—that we are all "watched over" by a "guardian angel." Nice notion. Kinda cute when ya think about it—little envoys of God out there hovering around and making sure nothing happens to us.

There's only one problem with that theory, I thought. If these little floating guardians are so busy, why do so many tragedies happen? Why were the Beatles allowed to break up? Why didn't my parents love me? That last one wasn't "me" in the sense of *me*, it was a figurative term.

And how about all those other bad things, like people dying and stuff like that? No, it just seemed too inconsistent. I was sure that we were all out

here in this cold world alone, left to fend for ourselves. My nickname in high school was "Scroogey"
by the way—and it wasn't because I had a wicked
knuckle ball.

Everything changed for me in the summer of
1986. It was the year I met my Guardian Angel.

Now I know that sounds hokey, especially coming from a meat-and-potatoes actor-director-sketch-
comedy type such as myself. But it did happen.

I was twenty-one at the time, living just
outside Eugene, Oregon. I had been wandering a
bit, trying odd jobs, really just marking time till
the residuals on my first commercial (Oxy-5—I
was the "before" guy) came through.

I had come into a lumberjacking job by the side
door—in other words, lying. They asked me if I
had any "jacking" experience, and I told them I
was the champion log roller from Kikajoo, Mon-
tana. They bought it. (Not to take anything away
from the folks up there, but let's just say if you've
got any city smarts, you can end up taking them
for a little trolley trip, no problem—if you catch
my scent.)

My first day at work found me literally pissing
my dungarees, strapped to a redwood trunk ninety
feet above the Columbia River Gorge. Too bad there
were three guys below me. I had no idea that these

people actually went up in trees and did things to them. In my naive mind, the image I always had was some burly guy in a red checked shirt with a big axe singing about his blessed blue ox, with his feet firmly planted on the ground.

But here I was, being yelled at from below by the men I had drenched, being told to "whittle the skiff" and "shunt the branches to their hard-nubs"—they might as well have been talking Chinese. Just as I was about to lose it—and add tears to the other fluids I had been releasing—a huge wind gust blew across the ridge we were on. It swayed the trees as if they were reeds, and I found myself almost parallel to the ground. An instant later I was swaying the other way. I clung on for dear life, sinking my practically nonexistent fingernails into the moist and supple bark. The men below me on the tree started chanting "Jock's toast! Jock's toast!"

In the panic of the moment, I immediately thought, "Oh man, what is this little 'inside term' they have, now?" Always with the "lumberspeak." I was jolted to reality with the dual realization that one end of my safety harness, bolted into the side of the tree, had come undone, and I was hanging only by the other one. It was as if I was a lure hanging off a deep-sea fishing rod, waiting to be cast.

Simultaneously, I realized that the men were referring to *me*. I had given a false name at the lumber mill. Jock Jocknell. I thought it would sound more like a woodsman. "Jock's toast!" was a reference to what I was about to become. Nice to know that lumberjacks stick together.

Before I could even process this info, another angry gust blew me the other way. This one was even more intense than the one before, and it yanked my one remaining bolt halfway out of the trunk. Now all that was holding me onto this wooden terror ride was a loose bolt and my now very sweaty palms. On the next gust I would surely be yanked from my perch and fall to a wealdy death, only to be laughed at by the macho lumber hands. They would probably enjoy crafting my pine death box, I thought, in a morbid moment of clarity.

My reverie was broken by that next gust. And sure as the hair rising on my buttocks, it lifted me clear off of that tree-turned-catapult, and I found myself flying free over the woods. There was a brief moment of silence as I watched the tool I had in my hand—I think it's called a saw—float down into the green thicket below me, not making any sound at all.

Then the trees were coming at me fast, and without mercy. I felt the pit of my stomach rise into my throat, and all I could think was that the Oxy-5 commercial would be the last known footage of me ever.

I closed my eyes tight, flailing my arms in front of my body reflexively. "*Noooo! Wahhhhhhh! Waaaaaahhhh!*"

"Stop crying like a little baby."

The voice came from everywhere and yet nowhere. I opened my eyes. I was hovering about ten feet above the sharp tip of the lower pine trees, about forty feet in the air. I had the strangest sensation—warm all over. At first I thought it might be the urine, but this was *all over me*. An incredible sense of well-being, as if I were being held, even fondled. But where was the voice coming from? Since I was being supported by this unknown force, hovering in space, I rolled over onto my back, facing the sky. So *this* is what it feels like to be in a helicopter, I thought.

Staring straight up at the cloudless sky, a form began to materialize above me. It was as if it were coalescing out of all the molecules in the nippy air surrounding me. It glowed a greenish blue light, and started to define itself as a humanlike form. First the head sprouted, without features, and then the body, large and rotund, and naked except for a loincloth.

As this form hovered over me, I forgot where I was. I only felt that this being above me was truly there to help me, and me alone. Slowly his facial features grew more defined—yes, it was a "he," that was for sure. His mouth was soft and friendly, surrounded by a dark day-old beard. His eyes were very familiar—round and open, and a little bit sad. I felt at once at ease with him, as if we had known each other for years.

The top of his head remained bald as a baby's, but his chest and belly were a thicket of dark undergrowth. Finally, from behind his back, two enormous feathered wings sprouted. They must have reached twenty or thirty feet across. Both glowed with that blue-green aura, flapping lazily behind him. It seemed like time had stopped, as I lay suspended in midair, beholding this large, very familiar-looking entity.

Finally, he belched. It echoed across the valley, the belch seeming to come, as his voice, from everywhere and nowhere, and I felt it pass through me. And for one glorious moment, I knew that I would be safe for the rest of my life. The feeling of rapture left as quickly as it had come, but the knowledge has stayed with me to this day.

"That was a close one, Stubby," he smiled.

"My name isn't Stubby."

"It is now. You will be and have always been Stubby in your heart. It's what I choose to call you, pardner."

The "pardner" is what tipped me off. The bald head, the huge body—of course! What had thrown me was the lack of a cowboy hat. I was sure that I had met this man before—but I hadn't. I only *felt* as if I had, because I had seen him on TV so much. It was Hoss, or the guy who played Hoss on *Bonanza*. Maybe it was the loincloth that had thrown me.

"I think I know who you are."

"I am the one who watches over you. I am your Guardian Angel."

"Aren't you Hoss, from *Bonanza*?"

"My name, if you wish to call me by one, is Hekezubiel."

"Really? Are you sure you aren't Dan "Hoss" Blocker?"

"I am Hekezubiel, your Guardian Angel, and you are Stubby."

"My name is Ben. And I could swear to—"

"—To who, pardner? You best watch your tongue, seeing as I hold your little life in my hands at this moment."

Just to bring home the point, he let me drop about five feet, which scared the living daylights out of me.

"Sorry . . . Hekezubius."

"Hekezubiel." There was a moment of awkward silence. I could tell he felt bad about having lost his temper with me.

"Look. Yes, I was on *Bonanza* at one point, in my earthly incarnation. But that was only a few seasons, and now I am your Guardian Angel."

I could tell that the TV show seemed to be a sore subject for him, so I let it go. Besides, I was feeling incredibly peaceful, and as gruff as his manner was, I really liked him. His presence filled me with golden lovelight that seemed to stem from an endless well.

"Why have you appeared to me?"

" 'Cause you were falling out of a tree."

Of course, I thought.

"I will always be your protector. I will always be there for you."

"Will I ever see you again?"

"I will never again come to you in an earthly vision. But you shall always feel my presence. Perhaps it will be in a dream, perhaps it will be in the way a certain odor comes to you in the middle of the day."

I began to weep. But not the tears of fear I had almost wept atop the tree earlier. No, these were tears of joy, of love and well-being. Hekezubiel/Dan "Hoss" Blocker *would* always be there for me. I knew it in the deepest reaches of my soul.

Slowly, I was falling to the ground—gently, as if on a cushion of air. I watched as he began to fade into the sky.

"Hey, isn't it ironic?"

He was almost gone now. All I could see was the dark outline of his back hair.

"What?" he called back. I could tell he was fading away fast, because now his voice seemed to come only from everywhere, as opposed to everywhere and nowhere.

"Just that, well you know, you're *actually* an angel, and Michael Landon played one on—"

I fell the last ten feet with a hard thud, flat on my back. I looked up to find all of the lumberjacks staring at me with confused looks. I stood up, unbuckled my tool belt, and walked out of that forest, never to return. To this day, I don't know what "whittling the skiff" means, though I do have some ideas.

Needless to say, my encounter with my guardian angel transformed my life. When I got back to New York, I immediately had my name legally changed to "Stubby Stiller." That lasted only a few months, until I realized there was a vaudeville comic by the same name registered in the actor's union. If I wanted to keep it I would have to become Stubby T. Stiller. (By the way, my middle name is *not* Tiberius, Trekkies!) I opted to go back to Ben.

But through the years, I have carried on a wonderful friendship with Hekezubiel. He communicates to me in all different ways, and is always encouraging my creativity. About a year after my encounter, I was inspired by him to write a movie based on our experience. It was entitled *My Angel*. Unfortunately, it was the same year that *My Bodyguard* hit the theaters, and my concept was deemed too "derivative." I guess they were afraid that audiences would get burned out on "My" movies.

Hek and I are practically inseparable. Whether he's communicating to me through an old *Bonanza* episode—which he does quite frequently—or just joining me on a plane trip cross-country (he likes to hang out on the wing, but he's no gremlin), we have become as close as an earthling and seraphim can be.

That's the wonderful thing about discovering your guardian angel. You realize that you're never alone. When I see a flick, Hek/Hoss is sitting right next to me—or on my lap if it's a horror picture. He laughs at my jokes and when I'm lonely, I just book a table for two at the most expensive French restaurant in town and Hek takes me out and treats me right. The best part of one of our angel's nights out is that I can drink all the bubbly I want and not have to worry driving home. I've got my guardian angel in the car, so it's zero to sixty and a little road fun, all under the watchful eye of my protector.

JANEANE

Eat, Drink and Be Scary

"He that lives upon hope dies farting."
—Ben Franklin
Poor Richard's Almanac, 1751

No longer a female-specific topic, corpulence and things that go in your mouth now concern the gents as well. I myself grapple with the "body shame/allowance of light during sex" conundrum frequently. Not that I'm sexually active, but I dwell on it nonetheless. Feeling shitty about your physique is an important state of mind, for it leads one into a series of diverse, unfulfilling relationships, as opposed to just one monogamous journey into the banal.[1]

---

1. In other words, if you hate you, you'll probably be able to enjoy a number of guys and gals who hate you, too. Chances are, you'll be very comfortable with that. So don't limit yourself to *one* bad, boring, insignificant other.

Let's begin by discussing dinner dates. This concept of traditional civilized courting bothers me. I, personally, don't want food interrupting my two grueling days of predate starvation.[2] (If I do dine out I want outrageously obscene amounts of food, and upscale restaurants rarely provide this. The quantities I'm referring to are best found on our supermarket shelf, taken home, and ingested quickly and shamefully, like the good Lord and the media intended.)

Dinner may confuse the issue. Let's assume the issue is one of lively conversation doused in liquor. Steaks and salad dilute the buzz essential to your being an active participant in a two-way conversation. Dialog, booths, and Stoli are the linchpins of a successful sexual liaison. Stilted mutterings over pasta primavera lead only to movies and a hasty car ride home. Conversely, feeling lean, mean, and hungry usually presages sex on the bathroom floor with the light on. This will give him/her the impression that you are freewheeling and above the brainwashing our supermodel culture has heaped upon us.

By skipping the meal, you may also spare yourself another grave indignity. Please do not be

---

2. See page 66. Don't do as I do, do as I say. Treat yourself right—eat some bread.

offended, delicate reader, by the path that I am about to take—gastrointestinal disorders.

My lower GI tract functions conspire in a cruel game of cat and mouse every time a potential sex partner enters the room. I can't even eat a Tic Tac without volcanic repercussion. I suspect that I am not alone in this vulgar, vulgar business.

My peer group has accepted this part of me graciously and with much good humor. But, curiously, the men in my life have failed to do the same. If you suffer as I do, perhaps you could tell your partner that your encroaching endometriosis only exacerbates an already regrettable situation.[3] This will work for either gender, as most people don't want to discuss it anyway. It is a sad fact that flatulence and sexuality mix like Susan Faludi and an Islamic Mullah, meaning that it is smelly and just plain wrong.

Hopefully you are not recoiling from this subject (bitter recrimination and finger-pointing will only incite the irritable bowel). It is my intention to aid, not to offend. The hour to discuss these issues is at hand. Many a great date has been sabotaged by the dreaded mix of "ethnic" foods and dark lagers.

If society wasn't so shortsighted, we'd have an

---

3. Ask your gynecologist. (Gentlemen need not ask their gynecologists.)

overabundance of happy, healthy couples. Instead we have young women slipping out of apartments like thieves in the night. The colon, she is a harsh mistress.

In summation, I'd have to advise you against eating[4] if you want to truly enjoy well-illuminated sexual relations and experience erotic pleasures unhampered by the intestine's fickle nature. The empty stomach will take you a lot farther on two tequila shots anyway, and your bank card will thank you in the morning.

---

4. Ignore page 188 and earlier footnote. Eat, don't eat—it's your call, based on your ability to "handle your business" when intoxicated.

JANEANE

Epilogue—
On Acting

As this book reaches its inevitable conclusion, it occurs to me that some of you are eager to hear what I have to say about thespianism.[1] (Ben Stiller's comments on this topic are tempered by the fact that his parents were grand champions on both *The $20,000 Pyramid* and *Tattletales,*[2] thereby insuring his smooth entrance into the family business.)

Perhaps you, too, would like to be an entertainer. Let me address your curiosity without the

1. Anyone interested in Renaissance fairs, Civil War re-creation, or song parody should consult *From Lilith to Ray Stevens* or *Guinevere Meets Gallagher*, both published by the Branson Commission for Family Fun.

2. Jerry Stiller's and Anne Meara's success on *Tattletales* brought them the respect of a very vocal group of Americans known as "The Banana Section." To this day, Ben counts on their support to "open" his films.

196 FEEL THIS BOOK

assistance of my trusty Sancho Panza, otherwise known as Vox Number One. I'll go it alone and let my head companion lie in wait for the next publisher to curry its favor.

I'll impart what I know of showbiz as succinctly as possible. I don't wish to overwhelm any would-be Jessica Tandys gamely paying their dues in local productions of *Showboat* or *Godspell*. There is always room for one more actor on the I-10 desperately racing to make that Budweiser "Volleyball Player #3" audition. A highway full of love has elastic lanes.

While it would be easy to say a dog run[3] is an apt metaphor for show business, it would be truer to say that show business is an apt metaphor for a dog run. Have you ever witnessed a tiny Jack Russell terrier[4] attempting to mount a larger breed? His earnest thrusting reveals both desperation and quasi-admirable chutzpa.

The larger dog shirking the diminutive interloper is an image that can represent many things in the vacuum-packed world of an actor. Each of us can conjure a scenario wherein we've played penetrator or penetratee. Occasionally we're granted the

---

3. Dog run: A segregated section of a public park dedicated to the needs of dogs and their predominately single owners.

4. The Jack Russell: a noted raconteur of the dog run. A favorite with the ladies until the constant yapping becomes exhaustive.

luxury of voyeurism so that we may view the other "dog" 's struggle. As we watch, a "there but for the grace of God go I" feeling washes over us. This brief encounter leering at the mounting pups allows us a much-needed dose of clarity. Clear thinking and reprioritizing lasts approximately two hours and occurs biannually. More often than not, we find our asses hopelessly linked within the doggy daisy chain yet again. Mantras are uttered and crystals are purchased to hasten the arrival of a benevolent bucket of water (a job) to be dumped upon our writhing bodies, allowing us to disengage.

You are free at last, until the job ends (or just your participation in it), and you wander off with your tail between your legs and no tennis ball. You drop exhausted beneath a bench until you corral the energy to chase your tail in circles again. How frequently this pattern repeats itself is as much of a mystery as that vaguely pornographic look on Larry King's face. So be careful, young reader. Do you really want to be an actor? Look again at the canine politics in your local dog park or kennel. After a focused evaluation, decide if Hollywood Boulevard is still an appealing sidewalk.

If the dog run isn't an appropriate example, let me try another tack. Reach back into your mental Rolodex of schoolyard games. Think of acting as one large Red Rover[5] game. Who gets "called over," and why, usually depends on one base thing. That one thing may expose your mother as a fibber—albeit well intentioned, but a fibber nonetheless.[6]

Unfortunately, looks are everything. Mom was trying to teach you something by asking you not to judge a book by its cover, but she failed to include an important caveat: Casting directors and producers aren't overly concerned with talent. They just need to know how much you weigh. So you see, Mommy had honorable reasons for leading you down the primrose path, but those reasons and her genetic coding can't help you now. Occasionally a "quirky"[7] type is called over, to pick up where Eve Arden left off.

In summation, let me extend the obligatory bit of advice: Work hard, believe in yourself, and never waver in your pursuit of excellence. Failing that, you should try: meeting Ben Stiller in a deli, bumping into Garry Shandling at a pilot taping, getting

---

5. Red Rover: A game wherein a group of children (often the bullies) form a chain. After arms are linked, they randomly summon or call over weaker, more naive children who have yet to be introduced to the culture of despair. The innocents race toward the human chain believing that good intentions are enough to break the wall of resistance.

6. See chapter on "The Ugly Truth." This is the second time I've called your mother a liar—what are you gonna do about it?

7. Usually a woman with dark hair who does not suffer from malnutrition.

dosed by a hot little New York gal with a tongue stud[8] and a lunchbox full of pills, having a psychotic break in front of apathetic strangers, making a movie with Uma Thurman, and cowriting a book. If none of the above seems appealing, I suggest reading *The Seven Habits of Highly Effective People*. I can't remember who wrote it.

---

8. Not to beat a dead horse, but the stud did add a new, textural eroticism to an otherwise tried-and-true act.

BEN

Ben's Last Chapter

I sit alone cuddled in a warm sheepskin comforter my Grampy sheared close to fifty years ago. I am on the front porch of my family's Wenokosha, New York, summer compound, rocking in a rocker in the dead of winter, and reading over the pages that you just have. As a lazy red toad of a sun sinks sallowly below the tree line, I can't help but smile at Janeane's sharp-tongued yet dead-on observations about life, or the mutual sparring session of our "He Said, She Said" contractual chapter. Yes, there's a lot there to feast on, and it helps if you're hungry.

An old raccoon we like to call "Shorty McBob" scampers across the huge expanse of front lawn that ambles lazily to our electrified fence, about an acre down the way. Pretty soon it will be dark and cold. I will retreat back to the city, where there are many distractions from the silence of being alone and with yourself.

I hope you have found these little stories and anecdotes as inspirational and enlightening as we have found writing them. If not, perhaps they made some of that inevitable water closet time pass all the more swiftly. As I pack up the manuscript, giving it the final once-over for typos and the like, my mind races through the miasma of memories and experiences that went into creating this book: all of the time spent on the phone with our agents, begging them to extend the deadline (such a *morbid* word!); months of pretending that it wasn't real, that maybe we could back out still; the cold hard realization and threat of legal action by our publisher that got our creative butts in gear; the begging and pleading with my writer "friends" to help me out in exchange for a nice hunk of dough; and finally, being forced to type away one painful key at a time on the old Mac until eventually, months later, we had fulfilled the minimum word count.

And then the joy and exultation of the completion of the writing process, perhaps the closest thing to a "holy" experience on this earth. I wouldn't trade it for the world.

As you head out into the world on your own journey, know that you are not alone, and that as long as there are lucrative book deals for people like us, you will never have to feel as if the world is a scary place where horrible things happen in random patterns with no meaning or sense of order.

Ooh. I just heard a little buzz and sizzle. Sounds like old Shorty tried to scamper off the property. That's my cue to pack it in.

Live With Passion!

Ben Stiller
Wenokosha, New York

BEN

Acknowledgment of Influences

In writing any book on relationships and self-knowledge, one is bound to draw upon many influences. In fact, you might argue that your entire life experience up to the moment of putting pen to paper is an influence. And if you argued that point, you might win—depending on how good an arguer you are. (See chapter 34!)

However, there are a number of books, plays, and movies that have strongly affected the content of this book. I will list them all here, often without reference to their authors, to whom I am forever indebted. I will also refrain from citing their specific influence on my writings regarding relationships and self-knowledge, as it seems to me they are all quite obvious.

Books

Deuteronomy
Crime and Punishment
The Hobbit
The Lord of the Rings
Errol Flynn's *My Wicked Wicked Ways*
Winnie the Pooh
A Billion for Boris
Donald Trump's *Art of the Deal*
The Pelican Brief
20,000 Leagues under the Sea
And anything by Tom Clancy!

Movies

Grand Theft Auto
Booty Call
The Poseidon Adventure
Houseguest
The Towering Inferno
Juggernaut
Cap'n Ron
The Swarm
Brian's Song
The Omega Man
The entire *Planet of the Apes* series, particularly
Beneath . . .

MUSIC

Music from *Miami Vice*—Various artists
"Meaty Beaty Big and Bouncy"—The Who
John Tesh's Tour de France Score
"Dancing Machine"—J5
"Bad, Bad Leroy Brown"—Jim Croce
"Emotion"—Samantha Sang
"All You Need Is Love"—The Beatles
"Eat My Foo Poppa Biddy Parts"—Pussmama G
and the Furious 2

To all the artists and writers and musicians who created these works—bravo! You have provided me with hours upon hours of distraction from other things I might have been doing, and in addition inspired me to get off my butt and do it, too!

Janeane's Glossary

BENNY'S BURRITOS. My favorite restaurant in New York.

BIBLE, THE. A marvelous work of fiction.

BROOKS, GARTH. Country megastar with terrible taste in shirts.

BURNS, ED and BAHNS, MAXINE. Two very pretty, very lucky people.

CHEKOV, ANTON. Heady playwright frequently referred to by Woody Allen.

COLUMBIA RECORD AND TAPE CLUB. Baby's first scam.

CRAWFORD, CINDY. Pathologically stiff public figure.

DANTE, ALIGHIERI. His *Divine Comedy* has provided me with many a reference for not-so-divine comedy.

FALUDI, SUSAN. Real gal's gal and provocative writer. Reminded us that the media is bothered by the vagina.

FRANKLIN, BEN. Diplomat, money model, inventor. Loved the ladies.

FRANZ, DENNIS. Popular actor with crusty exterior and soft, gooey, ratings-friendly middle.

FRAPPUCCINO©. Ambrosia of the Gods.

GAUGUIN, PAUL. Postimpressionist painter who makes me feel sad.

GINGRICH, NEWT; HELMSLEY, LEONA; THURMOND, STROM. Three people who don't give a tinker's damn about you or your next of kin.

GORTNER, MARJOE. Former evangelist and *Earthquake* star.

HILL, SAM. An expression, not a person.

HOLLYWOOD. *See* Starbucks.

HUMANA, VOX. Massive album for colonic enthusiast Kenny Loggins.

JONES, GEORGE. Country legend and Boris Yeltsin soulmate. Both men have a penchant for drinking vodka and disappearing for weeks at a time.

KIBBUTZ. Where to find "husband material."

LA GUARDIA, FIORELLO. Mayor of New York City and real can-do guy. Frequently referred to as "that fiesty little wop."

LIPNICKI, JONATHAN. Adorable moppet headed for a Tina Yothers adolescence.

MACHIAVELLI, NICCOLÒ. Wrote *The Prince*, which has been co-opted by history's biggest assholes as justification for some evil deed.

MALCOLM X. El-Shabazz, leader, philosopher, and Denzel Washington look-alike.

MASLOW, ABRAHAM. Psychoanalyst whose concept of the unattainable inspires apathy.[1]

MASON, JACKIE. Annoying comic who thrives on Jewish shtik.

MILL, JAMES. Thinker who leaned toward socialism, thereby arousing suspicion in many.

NANTUCKET AND ASPEN. The geographic answers to the philosophical question, "How many assholes can dance on the head of a pin?"

NIJINSKY. A turn-of-the-century dancer who was mightily proud of his "assets."

NORIEGA, MANUEL. Also know as "Pineapple Face." His adolescent angst is everyone's problem.

O'POOTERTOOT'S, T. J. Where the elite meet to eat.

ORWELLIAN UTOPIAS. Concept embraced by those who got their asses kicked in gym class.

---

1. Maslow may be a sociologist. It's difficult to write a book without a firm grasp on the facts such as they are.

PAGE, BETTIE. Red Hot Mama and post-punk icon.

PARKER, DOROTHY. A great writer and a hell of a witty drunk.

REED, RALPH. A man noted for his religious zealotry, girlish figure, and steadfast refusal to admit he has a crush on me.

REPUBLICAN NATIONAL CONVENTION. A fantasy getaway weekend for rich white guys, religious fanatics, self-hating women, and minorities.

RIDGELY, ANDREW. Former teen Wham!-er and a staple of VH-1 "Where Are They Now?" specials.

SCROTAL SAC. A region of the male anatomy that elicits laughter and, in some cases, pity.

SINN FEIN. The political arm of the Irish Republican Army. Ideological home to lots of cute Irish guys.

STARBUCKS. An institution that mocks the fact that I have too much time on my hands.

ST. VINCENT'S HOSPITAL. Institution in which I waited three and a half hours for salmonella treatment.

STILLER, BEN. Comic, actor, writer, and all-around underacheiver.

TILTON, ROBERT. Current evangelist. Has had his facial epidermis replaced with latex in order to attract viewers.

TOLSTOY, LEO. Fabulous writer who was appropriately depressed.

WHAT THE BUTLER SAW. Play written by that swinging London gay blade Joe Orton.

WOLSEY, CARDINAL. Former member of one of the most corrupt and monied global organizations.

WORLD'S GREATEST GRANDMA. I've been told that Jerry Seinfeld has a similar gag.

About the Authors

Ben Stiller and Janeane Garofalo are
currently touring the world, bringing their
unique message of enlightenment and hope to
seekers everywhere.